No Way To Live

NO WAY TO LIVE

Poor Women Speak Out

Second Edition

SHEILA BAXTER

Photos by Lori Gabrielson

New Star Books • Vancouver

Publication of this book is made possible by grants from the Canada Council, the Canadian Heritage Book Publishing Industry Development Program, and the Cultural Services Branch, Province of British Columbia.

Printed and bound in Canada
1 2 3 4 5   99 98 97 96 95
First printing of second edition, July 1995

Canadian Cataloguing in Publication Data
Baxter, Sheila, 1933-
  No way to live

  ISBN 0-921586-43-4
  1. Poor women — British Columbia — Case studies.   2. Women — British Columbia — Economic conditions — Case studies.   I. Title
HQ1459.B7B39 1994   362.83'09711   C94-910808-1

Acknowledgements

Thanks:

To all the women who contributed their thoughts to this book—without them it wouldn't have happened;

To Barbara Pulling, my editor, and to New Star Books for making it possible to publish this book;

To my supportive family and friends;

To all member groups of End Legislated Poverty, and to Jean and Sandy;

To Rita MacNeil, whose song "Flying On Your Own" inspired me many times as I worked on this book;

To Margaret D'Youville;

And to you, the reader—I hope that after reading this book you will want to join the fight to end poverty.

○

Contents

Introduction 11
Author's Note 16

1. Delilah · Mickey · Raven · Josephine · Rawnie ·
   Jewel · Mikiko · Rosa · How Poverty Affects My
   Kids 19

2. *Living on Welfare in B.C.: The GAIN Program* 48

3. Irene · Bessie · Patsy · Cathy · Edith · Donna ·
   Mabel · Robbie · Grace 60

4. *Poverty and the Common Woman* 76

5. Jackie · Tracy · Sybil · Doreen · Gus · Tina ·
   Angela · Daphne · Micheline · Helga 83

6. *Working as a Welfare Advocate* 101

7. *The System From Inside: A Social Worker's
   Perspective* 132

8. Linda · Dana · Ellen · Star · Leah 138

9. *Fighting Child Poverty* 153

10. Nicole · Farendias · Kathryn · Sheila 164

11. *The Lighter Side of Poverty* 174

12. Shirley · Josie · Fanny · Antoinette · Jean ·
    Anne · Lorna 184

13. *Single Moms and Social Change* 198

14. Lise · Frieda · Ursula · Audrey · Yvonne ·
     Diana 208

   Appendix 1 Ending Poverty: Some Ideas 225

   Appendix 2 Anti-Poverty and Women's
     Groups 230

O

To all women everywhere who are struggling with poverty

Introduction to the First Edition

In 1986, I spent more than two months on the streets of Vancouver, interviewing poor women. It was a hot summer, but the women I spoke with could not get out of the city. They could not afford to get out of the city. Many could not even afford bus tickets. We talked and talked. Some of the women wrote down their thoughts:

"Welfare sucks."

"My solution to poverty is suicide."

"I am sure that I will always be poor."

Click . . . click . . . click.

In the game of Russian roulette, there are always losers. Our system, in which the women I interviewed are trapped, is like that deadly game. Few of them, unfortunately, will make it.

Welfare rates in British Columbia, where I did my research, are as much as 50% below the poverty line. Poverty is growing in the province, and we now have more than a quarter of a million people living on welfare or unemployment insurance, and tens of thousands more are paid wages that keep them below the poverty line.

I am poor myself, and as I worked at this book I struggled with low self-esteem. "Who are you and what right do you have to work on and publish such a book?" I asked myself. Even after I had done the interviews, my lousy self-esteem kept saying, "You can't do it. You can't do it . . . "

But I was angry. Poor women have a right to be heard. Government, special commissions, churches, and academics have spent millions of dollars trying to understand poverty and the poor—but how often were the poor themselves consulted, listened to?

I asked the women I talked to three basic questions: What are the reasons for your being poor? What could be done to change your situation? and Do you think you will always be poor?

They let me into their minds sometimes for only a couple of minutes, and then the door closed. Their thoughts are often short. The replies came on the street, over the phone, or in community centres and shelters. They were given verbally or written on the form I supplied; in some cases, women chose to write a short article about their experiences. I spoke to women of many different ages and races. But there were common denominators. Women wanted not handouts, but education, opportunity, civilized living at reasonable rent, an end to prejudice.

The most common problem seemed to be the very one which afflicted me throughout this work—a lack of self-worth, of self-esteem. The reason for this, the women said in varying ways, was society's attitude towards them. They felt that being poor, or having a psychiatric history or a criminal record, meant that they were outcasts. They felt they had been judged. One woman said, "This is a throw-away society, and I have been thrown away." Another woman said, "Not all the blame should go to the system, but it is often hard to see where it should go when you are too hungry to think straight."

Many said, "No one has ever asked me about my life before." No one ever asks poor women anything much. They are told what to do, directed, controlled. The women I spoke with were Black, white, Asian, Native Indian. They ranged in age from eighteen to over sixty-five. They were both lesbian and heterosexual, and they held a variety of political beliefs. Some had university degrees, others had limited education. Some were in poor states of physical and mental health; others were reasonably healthy. But they were all women, and all poor. I was respected and trusted by them because of my work as a welfare advocate.

Many other studies, I feel, have been tokenism, providing entertaining stories which show the poor as negative people who are unmotivated and somehow just don't want to work. The interviews which follow are presented in as unedited a way as possible—and they explode that myth. What the women say they need are free bus passes, free education, real job training, and real jobs which pay a living wage. They say workers in social service offices do not listen to them enough—they feel they are often treated as stupid or deviant. They want good, safe housing, a clothing allowance, recreational opportunities. They want dignity and respect in their lives.

This material is not entertaining. It's not meant to be. Some of it is repetitive, but poverty *is* boring and repetitive. You may find yourself getting bored as you read this book, bored with the sameness of the women's problems and the solutions they suggest. Take that bored feeling, multiply it a million times, and you will begin to get a sense of how boring it is to be forcibly poor.

Most of the women I interviewed live in the Downtown Eastside or the East End of Vancouver. But poor women live in many different neighbourhoods and in many different situations. Some of us live in hotels or rooming houses or on the street, others in housing co-ops or cheap apartments. Many of us depend on welfare to support ourselves and our children. Others are "working poor"; our jobs provide us with incomes that are sometimes slightly higher, sometimes lower than we would receive on welfare.

The unemployment rate in B.C. at the beginning of this year was 11.4%. For women, the rate is always higher: in January 1988, approximately 12.2% of the women who wanted to find work outside the home were unable to do so. But even though jobs are scarce, there is a persistent myth that the unemployed simply do not try hard enough. The attitudes which lay behind the English Poor Laws established in the 1600s are still held today by those in authority. Then, the "able-bodied poor," people who were considered to be responsible for their own poverty, were severely punished if they didn't work or if they begged. Three hundred and eighty-eight years later, people are still punished for being unemployed. Unemployed workers in B.C. who receive welfare under the Guaranteed Available Income for Need (GAIN) program are classified as "employables." They get reduced welfare payments and no free medical coverage, and are regarded as lazy deviants. Their joblessness is seen as their fault.

Since I started work on this book, things have gotten even worse for poor women. In B.C., the Vander Zalm government continues its attack on poor people with more cutbacks in social services, a proposed restructuring of the welfare system, threats to apprehend children from poor families, an illegal attempt to exempt abortion from medicare coverage, and a new "strengthen-the-family" program which will further restrict the options available to women in the province. And both the proposed free trade agreement with the U.S. and privatization, on a provincial and a national scale, will only make poor women poorer, through the erosion of social services, fewer jobs and lower wages.

Society must accept that poverty is a social problem, not a personal one. Most of the women I interviewed said that their *biggest* problem was the attitude society shows towards them when they become poor or sick. The issues surrounding welfare and unemployment must be faced, talked about, dealt with. Solutions must be found.

Many of the women I talked to were hungry, broke and very tired. As I sat at a women's drop-in centre one day with three women who had agreed to be interviewed, a fourth woman came in. She had just spent the last of her money on a can of sardines. She shared it. One of the centre's volunteers made some soup, and the women ate it hungrily. It was the middle of the month; cheque day was a long way off. They shared the meal, as they shared their thoughts with me. I am indebted to them all. Here is what the poor women of one community have to say, interspersed with stories taken directly from my welfare advocacy work, and statistics which show that the problems these women face are common to poor women around the province and across the country.

As the women wrote or talked, their anger showed. In clenched hands, bent heads, eyes that blinked back tears, heads thrown back in defiant anger, and in hurt that was stifled. Then a blank staring into space, as painful memories flooded the mind.

Poor women, stuck in a game of Russian roulette.

You get sick. Click.

You lose your job. Click.

You get depressed. Click.

You are in an accident. Click.

You go to prison. Click.

Your husband leaves you and the kids. Click.

You leave your husband. Click.

Click...click...click.

This is no damn way to live.

Sheila Baxter
Vancouver, B.C.
April 1988

O

Author's Note

I met most of the women I interviewed for this book while I was working as a volunteer at a downtown women's centre. I also approached women I knew through friends or other political groups. But as a poor woman, my time and resources were very limited, and that meant I couldn't talk to as many women as I wanted to. I am especially sorry not to have been able to interview any women working as farmworkers or in the garment trade, two areas of notorious exploitation, and I would have liked to meet with women who live outside the centre of the city in suburban or rural areas. To all the women whose experiences are not represented here, I hope there will be more books like this where you can talk about your poverty and be heard.

Wherever possible, each woman's racial or ethnic background is given with her story. Sometimes, though, I didn't feel comfortable asking for this information, either because I didn't know the woman I was interviewing or because our conversation was very brief, and it seemed too personal a question. So where the woman herself has not supplied this information, it is not provided.

Both lesbians and heterosexual women were interviewed for the book, so a woman may be talking about either a woman or a man when she refers to her lover or partner.

The majority of women who appear here wanted to remain anonymous, so in most cases the woman's name and some minor details of her story have been changed. The photos in the book are of women from the community where I worked, but not of the actual women interviewed.

Finally, a note about the use of the term "poverty line" throughout the book. In Canada there are three major poverty lines used to make statistical calculations about poor people. Both the National Council of Welfare and Statistics Canada use a budget-based approach, defining the low income cut-off point as the point at which more than a certain percentage of gross income is spent on food, shelter and clothing. NCW sets this point at 56.2%, StatsCan at 54.7%. The Canadian Council on Social Development uses a relative income approach, establishing the poverty line at 50% of an average Canadian family income as estimated by Statistics Canada. See page 55 for a comparison of established poverty lines.

In interviewing women for this book, I have considered them to be living below the poverty line if they do not have enough money to meet their basic needs or those of their families.

. . .

It's seven years on now, and for the most part there are the same problems . . . same pain, same struggles, day in and day out. There are a few new resources. There is a tad more social housing and some women are really happy to be in safe housing, but there are so many who are on various waiting lists, in transition houses. Personally, I don't see much change. We have a New Democratic government in B.C., and it did raise the minimum wage and the GAIN rates, but not to the point where recipients are living above the poverty line. The NDP shuffled ministries so that the former Ministry of Social Services and Housing (MSSH) is now the Ministry of Social Services (MSS) (both acronyms are used in this book), but they are continuing the Social Credit tradition of welfare-bashing, accusing people on welfare of making fraudulent claims and cheating the system.

For this new edition I updated the statistics and tables. In the interviews I didn't change references to GAIN rates and minimum wage; these are still given as the 1987-88 figures.

However, current GAIN rates are shown in the table on page 50 and current minimum wage rates are on page 53. The monthly budgets on pages 51 to 53 show how far GAIN or minimum wage will go to cover average families' living expenses in 1995.

I've kept in touch with some of the women I interviewed in 1987-88, and there have been changes in their lives too. The little one in the photo on page 162 died of a brain tumour. His mom was devastated. She came to see me, to see a copy of the book. I gave her one. She said it was the only picture she had of her son . . .

One woman who had a small apartment in the east end of Vancouver got sick and went into hospital. When she came out, her apartment had been rented to someone else. She was placed in a hotel near Main and Hastings, in a room over the bar, in the middle of the drug and sex trade. She couldn't survive there, and committed suicide. The community had a memorial for her. Her friend, a social worker, said that poverty killed her.

There have been positive changes too. Raven is very politically active. Her son is grown up now, and she has freedom to choose her career as a volunteer activist. I've interviewed her for all my books now, and she's committed to fighting poverty.

I wish that after seven years I didn't need to reprint this book but, since I do, I hope it will empower you, the reader, to take political action against poverty, because poverty is political.

1.

Delilah

Delilah is a twenty-eight-year-old Black woman with a welfare income.

I feel that being poor is not just a physical reality; it's a state of mind at the worst. I am an individual person, part of a family, being forced to fit a peg or classification in a system that makes no allowances for individuality. Our needs as a family are not considered to any reasonable degree at all.

Financial aid workers often do not try to work with you within the confines of the system, your needs being totally unimportant to them. Often you are told that the worker has no time to deal with something, or that she doesn't know anything about it. Very rarely do you ever encounter anyone who makes an active effort to work with you and understand the individual needs of your family. Not all the blame should go to the system, but it's often hard to see where it should go when you are too hungry to think straight.

I personally am poor because the man who supports me is in jail for a crime that he did not commit but only had knowledge of, not a crime of violence or hate. Unfortunately, society could not find a way for this man to remain in the community and support his family while paying his debt to society. Now the taxpayers support him, paying for his room and board and his medical and dental bills in addition to supporting myself and my child, paying our room and board, our dental and medical, etc.

Poverty is a lack of understanding of people's needs,

as opposed to wants. It begins on the most basic level
with a mistaken assumption that we can exist on the
basic social assistance rates. It is mistakenly assumed
that you, the parent, can rent a decent place to live and
provide a clean, bright, healthy environment with
nutritious meals and clean clothes on the amount of
money provided. People on welfare try harder and hus-
tle more to care for their children, clean the house, and
do laundry in the bathtub because there is not even
enough money to go to the laundromat. It is hard when
the mother is not receiving a proper diet.

This could be changed by the people of the community working together with the government to set up realistic guidelines that we could work within. A clearer
understanding of the needs of the people in the community can be obtained by asking them! A great deal of
money need not be wasted setting up a committee of
government employees to look into this matter—just
ask anyone who has had to struggle to survive on basic
subsistence rates. Given sixty days of daycare and a bus
pass, I personally could get off and stay off welfare forever. But although this sounds like a reasonable request, it does not fall within their guidelines in my
case, and so I will never get it. It's not as though I
don't know what I need. God knows I have spent
enough time just sitting in my house planning what I
need to remove myself from this trap. I'm angry!!! They
give me my cheque so grudgingly every month, as
though it causes them physical pain to talk to me, but
they hold me back and refuse to provide the things that
I need to remove myself from this trap—the welfare
trap.

O

Mickey

Mickey is a forty-three-year-old woman in poor health. Her income is from GAIN. She has a Grade 12 education, and has worked in the hotel business. She would like to take some college courses.

I am poor because of bad health, the way the system works, the lack of encouragement for girls to go into "masculine" fields when I wanted to. When I went to school, I was given no support in the choices I made, which were considered masculine. Times have changed now.

I have no idea as to whether I will always be poor. Welfare should provide more incentives for people to get jobs, instead of punishing you for working—for example, deducting the money you make from part-time work from your cheque. Social workers should treat their clients like citizens instead of second-class people.

O

Raven

Raven is a thirty-nine-year-old Native woman. She is a single mother who lives on a welfare income. She has taken humanities courses at a local community centre, and wants to continue her education.

I think I'm poor because of society. The politicians and their attitudes. They figure we should always be volunteers and not get paid. High rents with no controls cut into my food budget. The quality of housing you can get when you're poor is bad. People discriminate against single mothers, too. You are not a family if you don't have a husband! To buy enough food, you have to do housecleaning for other people and get paid under the table. There's a lot of mothers doing it. It's the only way they are able to survive. People are not lazy—they are struggling.

Many things need to be changed:

1. Raise welfare rates. Don't divide welfare into shelter and support—make it one amount. Now, if you do locate a cheap place, the extra money is stopped off your cheque. You should be rewarded, not punished, if you find a cheaper home. Welfare increases should not be taken by greedy landlords. There should be legislation to stop this happening. The amount welfare recipients can earn to supplement their welfare should be increased. If the poor were given more to live on, this would cut down on our hospital costs.

2. Stop apprehending children of the poor. Social workers should not be allowed to interfere with families unless there is definite proof of neglect or abandon-

ment. Most of the kids in care are poor. We need to give kids on welfare the same rights as children in foster care, who get clothing allowances, money for hobbies, bus fare. Society should show more respect for poor kids.

Family court cases should be investigated by an independent body. At the present time, one parent is moved out while they cover up for the other. The child is destroyed by the present system.

Family court should allow the parents to choose their own psychologist, as many of the government's psychologists are really "out to lunch."

3. To make people feel good about themselves, offer courses in parenting skills, community activity, payment for community volunteer work. New clothes would also help.

4. Treat us with dignity and respect at the welfare office. Some workers discourage recipients from asking for their rights. I've seen it happen time and time again.

5. Raise the minimum wage to at least $6.00 an hour. Give people incentive to work. You can't live on $4.00 an hour [the current minimum wage for adults in B.C.; for those aged sixteen to eighteen, the minimum wage is $3.65]. Stop age discrimination against young people: they work just as hard. We don't want slave labour.

6. Change society's attitude towards the poor. They should start listening to the victims, support them, not condemn them as "welfare bums," "welfare families." My son was called "Welfare Wally" by his school peers.

7. Every politician should have to survive on welfare for six months, and live in substandard housing.

Poor people have lost faith in politicians and society. They are often so run-down emotionally and physically they don't even vote. The poor must change their attitudes: they have to stop attacking each other and begin to support each other. Frustrations should be directed at the people who are causing the situation. When we fight each other, it lets the politicians off the hook. The poor must organize and band together, like they did in the 1930s Depression. Write letters and petitions to politicians. Let them know how you feel.

I had parents and grandparents that gave me love and support. That has helped me stay well. I have not had to use alcohol and drugs as a crutch. Some people have to, because of circumstances in their life.

I think I will always be poor, unless there are some drastic changes made. There is a large profit in keeping people poor. Being part Native and a woman is another reason I shall always be poor. Discrimination for jobs and housing is faced on a daily basis.

At my community centre where I do volunteer work, I have been told that Native people should not be allowed in. They say we should use the Indian Centre. My argument is that a community centre is for everyone, especially the poor. It is just a few ignorant ones who have this attitude but it can make your life miserable. Keeping people of different races divided gives the politicans more power.

O

Josephine

Josephine is over sixty-five years of age. She is politically active in the area of pensioners' rights.

Even senior women who get a GAIN supplement to their old age pension live way below the poverty level. Many have just toast and tea for meals. They often can't afford good, nutritious food; tea and toast stops the hunger and it's easy to make. Many women are ashamed to admit they are poor because their generation kept these things hidden.

User fees for health care services and prescription fees that can run as high as $15 make things very difficult for seniors. The tax on long distance calls also hits us, because with relatives and children in other provinces, that's how we keep in touch.

The government takes money away from seniors, the most vulnerable group in society. They keep eroding what we already have. Rights that we won are disappearing. They think we can't fight. We can still vote, though!

Do I think older women will always be poor? Well, I don't see things getting any better. I don't see any improvement; we can't even keep what we've got.

Changes I'd like to see:

All recreation centres for seniors should serve one good meal a day.

User fees must go.

A real cost of living index should be built into our pensions. The present one is not accurate.

The basic old age pension should be increased.

The homemaker service [a government-subsidized program which provides assistance to older people and disabled people in their homes] must be expanded. At the moment, you go on a waiting list just to be evaluated.

There should be rent controls and more tenants' rights.

We need social housing for seniors now—our time is running out.

O

Rawnie

Rawnie is a white woman in her early thirties.

Maggie and I go back a long way. We went to university together, and lived in the same apartment block there. When I moved into this housing co-op, she moved into it, too. We've sat at the kitchen table many nights sharing feelings about being single parents, studies we've either read or are writing, and being on welfare. In all the years I've known her, she had never given me reason to doubt her, but, well, she had just told me something very odd.

"You're kidding!" I said in disbelief.

Maggie repeated again how much she hated going into the MSSH [Ministry of Social Services and Housing] office and having to talk to the receptionist. After talking to her, my friend insisted, she felt so scorned, put-down, and humiliated that she wanted to go home and cry.

"The receptionist treats me like I can't be trusted," she continued. "Like the only reason I need help is because I'm a moral degenerate. Like I've actually come to steal the stapler or something."

"How odd," I commented. "I've always thought she was a real sweetheart. When I come, she remembers my name, talks directly to me, and sees to my problem right away. She has always been thoughtful and efficient with me."

Maggie started to smile. "That, my dear, is because you use a wheelchair and have difficulty with co-ordination and hearing. You are quite visibly disabled.

27

You are, as they say, one of the 'deserving poor.'"

I wondered if maybe it also had something to do with the fact that the first time I talked to the receptionist, I pressed up to the counter to try to hear her, knocked over her papers, and, when she came out to pick them up, accidentally ran over her foot.

I had to agree that Maggie was probably right. I remembered once when I thanked the receptionist for doing something for me, she said, "That's what I'm here for," and I got the distinct impression that she thought I was *supposed* to be on welfare. Most of society undoubtedly feels the same way. Many's the time I have applied for a job and been told that I was a brave little thing but that I really needn't work at all. That I should just stay on welfare, that I should "relax and accept it." Or was it "lie back and enjoy it"? I wasn't sure, but it didn't really make much difference anyway.

A nightmarish courtroom scene flashed through my mind:

"Will the prisoner please rise and face the bench? How say you, ladies and gentlemen of the jury?"

"Guilty, your honour! Guilty of being a disabled woman!"

"Thank you, jury members!" Turning back to me, the judge thunders, "You have heard the verdict. I therefore sentence you to poverty and a morass of bureaucratic hassles and sexism masquerading as charity...for life!"

As I am bound in red tape and led away sobbing, he feels a little sorry about the harshness of the sentence and calls out to me in a conciliatory voice: "I further decree that you shall be considered to be one of the Deserving Poor and that receptionists will be polite to you!"

Maggie's voice broke into my reverie: "...like it's okay for you to ask for help," she was saying. "Disabled people even get a bit more money."

"The reason we get more money is because it costs

more money to be disabled. Many drugs, pain treatments, special diets and equipment are not covered by MSSH but are necessary anyway. So we get a little more to pay for it ourselves. It's not enough, though. Our standard of living actually falls below yours."

I noticed the "you/us" dichotomy that had crept into our conversation, so I said forcefully: "It's really the same thing, you know. I mean, the 'logic' of welfare puts both of us into exactly the same prison. Welfare payments are so low, and the whole system is so wretched, that people are supposed to think any job at all is preferable to not working. The idea is to squeeze us back into the labour force. But, when for one reason or another—the ages of our children, our health, society's attitude towards us, or whatever—we *cannot* work, we are still treated as if we *will* not work."

"Well, I won't be staying in this prison forever!" she asserted. "As soon as my youngest is in daycare, I'm getting out. I'll have my degree. I'll get a high-paying full-time job and buy my kids a good education so they won't ever be stuck like this."

I wondered privately how realistic that was but said nothing to her, letting her enjoy her daydream. Still, I realized that it was a daydream that I—and a lot of disabled women like me—could not share in, even in theory. It was time to go, but as I was leaving I turned to her: "One last question?"

"Shoot," she nodded.

"Why?"

"Why what?"

"Why do disabled women 'deserve' to be poor?"

O

Jewel

Jewel is a twenty-nine-year-old white woman with a welfare income. She is in poor health.

I am poor because of no education, no real jobs, and wrong decisions in my life.

To change my situation there would have to be more real jobs, free education, better governments, more recognition of women's rights and problems, and more money to live on.

I hope I won't always be poor. I want to get more education, a steady job, and a good future in the long term. Sadly, the short term is almost unliveable.

O

Mikiko

Mikiko is a Japanese-Canadian woman in her mid-thirties.

I'm poorer now that I'm working than when I was on welfare. I'm making approximately $1,200 a month gross, but now I'm supporting my husband and myself, with no medical coverage. We don't get premium medical or premium dental like we did on GAIN; we don't get nothing. We're paying rent that is $350, which was easy when I was on welfare because I never saw the money, but now I have to take it out of my pocket and pay it and it's really hard. Luckily, I don't have to pay for a bus pass; I only live two blocks from work. I'm working on auxiliary, so I don't get a whole lot of hours.

When I started working I thought, geez, now I can afford to buy other people things. Like people in my co-op, single mothers who are broke at the end of the month, I would go out and buy them some groceries and stuff. Now it's getting really expensive and I can't afford to do it anymore.

I never want to go back on welfare. Self-esteem while you are on welfare is really low. You end up being dependent on somebody you don't want to be dependent on. You don't have any say or any control over your own life. When I was a single parent on welfare and my kids were here, welfare was always checking up on me, social workers were pulling these short-notice visits, like five minutes notice, to see who was living at my house. To see whether I was living with my ex-husband, who was my husband at that time.

Even when I wasn't on welfare, a social worker from St. Paul's Hospital came and tried to talk me into giving up my youngest daughter for adoption. I was on the methadone program when she was born and I had cut myself down to 10 mg. a day which is just minimum, the lowest you can take and not be sick, but the worker tried to talk me into giving my daughter up.

In my books, to live on welfare is the worst thing in the world. I don't care if I have to work another job for $4.00 an hour to support my husband and I for the rest of my life, I never want to go back on welfare. There's a lot of advantages to being on welfare; you don't have to pay your medical and you don't have to pay your dental. But they have too much control. The government, in the end, runs your life. You don't have a say in anything that you do.

I was first involved with social workers when I was a runaway. When I was twelve I had run away to Winnipeg and I was in the Youth Centre there for four months because I wouldn't tell them who I was or how old I was, or anything like that. They finally found out who I was and sent me home. A social worker met me at the airport and apprehended me right there. When I was fifteen, because I didn't want to live at home, they got a court order to put me in a psychiatric unit for a month, welfare did, and really messed up my life. Tried to put me on chlorpromazine for a year and all this other garbage. So I ran away and I came out here.

I completed my G.E.D. [General Education Diploma] last year. I have my Grade 12 now. I have no training yet, but I plan on going to school. I want to get into early childhood education, to work with kids— young kids, babies and toddlers and pre-school kids—and teach them alternatives to being abused children. Just teach them things so that they don't have to go through what I had to go through. Like, if their parents are beating them, then I want to be able to teach them that they can go for help and somebody will be supportive.

When somebody is sexually molesting them, get them to where they can say, hey, he's touching me and I don't like it. Help them work out their skills. A lot of the kids that I've worked with in this area are really angry because of the abuse, physical and sexual. They work it out with anger. They're really hostile and they're really violent, and if you don't help them work through that, then they are going to end up being really hostile, angry adults.

I know a lot of the street people around here. About 90% of them come from poor homes. I know women working the street now whose mothers were hookers because they were poor and whose grandmothers were hookers because they were poor. To work the street is just another way to stop from being poor. When I worked the street, I did it because I didn't want to have to go on welfare. That's the only reason that made me go out there. I guess I was poor, but I knew there was always a way to get money. If I was hungry I could go out and turn a trick, or if I wanted to buy something new, I could go out and turn a trick and come up with the money. Men'll pay anywhere from $20 to $200. One guy that I used to take out from City Hall would pay $130 an hour. That's a lot of money. My rent at that time was $375 a month and that was a good portion of it.

I turned tricks when I was a kid to get my education. I was a child in care here in Vancouver when I was sixteen. I took off from this group home. I went out and turned a trick, couple tricks. I got an apartment and I turned a couple more tricks, bought groceries and paid for my school books and stuff. That's how I went to school for the full year of Grade 10. I turned tricks the whole time I was going to school.

There's the poor and the middle-class who understand what it's like to be poor, and then we have the people who haven't got the *foggiest* idea of what it's like to live in poverty. People that live in rich areas and

own houses and have 2.5 kids and drive two cars,
right? They don't have the slightest idea of what it is
like. These guys who come down here driving Porsches
and antique Corvettes prey on women who live in
poverty, picking them up and beating them up and taking advantage of them.

I have a home, and if I have a home, then people that
don't have a home and are in crisis should have a place
where they can go and be safe and be warm and have
sleep and not be harassed. So, that's what my home is.
My home is like a crisis centre in this area. People have
buzzed my door at three and four in the morning saying they need a place to crash, they can't go home or
they don't have a place to go, and I'll take them in.

Like Jo. Jo is twelve. A street worker came in one day
when I was at work and said that he needed a favour of
me. If this guy needs a favour then I know it's something important. He told me he had a young girl who
had been turned out in the street and needed a place to
stay until she could get a few things straightened out.
So Jo stayed at my place for five days and she's coming
back next week.

I don't get paid for taking her in like a foster parent
would. You know, it would be nice to have money to
spend on her but that's not what's important. What's
important to me, like I told Jo when I first met her, is to
make sure that she is safe and that she's fed.

She's an amazingly mature twelve-year-old, physically
and mentally. She looks about fifteen or sixteen and I
have to keep reminding myself that she is only twelve
years old. She comes from a family that has split up.
Her father lives out here and her brother lives out here
and her mom and her stepdad live in the interior of
B.C. Her stepfather has beaten on her; her stepfather
has tried to sexually abuse her. That's when Jo took off.
When her stepfather tried to sexually abuse her she
decided it was time to leave. She came to Vancouver
and was victimized, that's the best word I know for it,

by another woman and two guys who preyed on her because she was naive. I don't think she'll go back out and work the street. I stressed to her while she was staying with me that if she wanted to work that had to be *her* decision. I told her that nobody has the right to force her out on the street and if people tried to force her out on the street, then she should leave.

How can it be a fair system when the rich keep getting richer and the poor keep getting poorer and the people that suffer are the children and the mothers and the fathers? You know, I'm surprised there aren't more suicides in this area, from the depression of having to live on welfare and depend on a government that wins votes by saying, "We'll do this kind of social reform" and "We'll make your life a lot easier" and then they forget about you when they're elected. You know, like we were promised an increase in welfare rates. What happened? It's still almost the same amount it was a few years ago. How can a person survive on these welfare rates from one month to the next? The government has to understand what poverty is really like, and they have to do something to stop it.

One way would be to give people more money, larger support portions on their welfare cheques. Another thing would be affordable housing. To heck with shelters—it's just the rich getting richer off the poor.

As far as I'm concerned, there's got to be a subsidy for people that are working and making really lousy wages. People that are working, like I'm working, are still poor and there's got to be some kind of subsidy, some kind of help. If you are only making $800 or $900 a month then you should be able to get subsidized for your medical and your dental. That's supposed to be happening now, but I was on that subsidy and I just got a bill for $52.

I'd like to see education be a priority because I know for me completing my G.E.D. gave me the incentive to go out and look for work. Since I got my G.E.D., I've had two different jobs. I've been unemployed for a grand total of seven weeks. I have been working steady for the last year because I got part of my self-esteem back by finishing my Grade 12 and doing things for me. Welfare wouldn't even help me pay for my G.E.D. I had to pay for that out of my own pocket.

In a sense, I think I'll always be poor because I'll always be helping other people out. You know, like the women at my co-op—if they're broke, then I'll always be there for them. But I believe that I've got my goals set in my life now, and it's going back to school and it's getting my Early Childhood Education certificate. This is the first time in my life I've decided what I really want to do, and I'm going to do it.

O

Rosa

Rosa is a forty-three-year-old woman who was born in Spain. She is in poor health. Her income is from welfare.

I wasn't always poor. I was a secretary, I managed a store and I also taught at a college. I became very sick—I had a serious heart attack and never got better. I will always be poor because I am sick.

If I had enough money, I would like to buy some art equipment to do art work. I am very angry. I feel that society has pushed me aside. Thrown me away. If I had something important to do...if there were more free recreation...if only welfare would be acceptable to society. My hopes are on a new government.

O

How Poverty Affects My Kids

The following letter was read at the Child Poverty Forum held in Vancouver in April 1987.

I guess for me it is a little easier because I am married. I have my husband beside me. He had a fair paying job with the city until the cutbacks started. When he was laid off, we were waiting for the arrival of our third child. We were devastated. We hoped that before the baby was born, he would be back to work. Boy, were we wrong. We now have three children, two girls ages sixteen and three years, and one son age eight. It has been three years since my husband has had any steady employment. He has had odd jobs, but nothing ever seems to be permanent.

I think the first year was the hardest to deal with on welfare. We had to get used to living on a fixed income of $798 per month. Thank God for B.C. Housing [government-subsidized housing available to a small number of low-income people]. Our rent is at least reasonable—$217 a month. After we pay our utilities there never seems to be enough left over for food or clothing. I am becoming very adept at shuffling money. The old adage "Steal from Peter to pay Paul" is true. It's tough. It's really tough. Once we get our cheque at the end of the month, we have food in the house for about two weeks and then it's gone. So is the money. So many nights I put the kids to bed and they are saying, "But Mom, I'm still hungry." It just breaks my heart to watch

them go to the fridge and leave it empty-handed. Or to
grab a carrot and run it under water to see if it will
stiffen up. By the end of the month there is usually
only carrots and onions left in the fridge; all the good
stuff has long been eaten. The milk lasts about two to
two and a half weeks, and then that's it for the rest of
the month. Same with the eggs and cheese. The fruit
usually lasts one week. Canned goods last a little longer, and thank God for the food bank; they make things
go a little bit farther. The powdered milk helps, for baking and things. My kids just can't seem to make themselves drink it, so I usually only use it for cooking. I
brought them up on good milk and no matter how hard
I try to make them drink the powdered stuff, they still
choke and cry and carry on. They will take it in their
cereal if I can mask it with a little extra sugar or cinna-
mon. My son has gone to school many a morning crying because I made him eat the cereal with "that milk"
on it. I'm sorry, honey, I try.

We try to budget the money, but no matter how hard
we try there just doesn't seem to be enough to feed my
growing family, not nutritionally anyhow. They are
good kids. They hardly ever complain, but I can see it
in their faces when I give them "instant noodles again!"

My eldest daughter turned sixteen in December. Also
in December, she decided to quit school. She has been a
troubled child for a few years now. One of her reasons
for quitting was clothing. She felt very uncomfortable
going to school in "those holey jeans." Let's face it,
even when I went to school there was that competition
on who's wearing what. It's still there, even though
now it is blue jeans and T-shirts. Those jeans are expensive, as are the runners they wear. She couldn't compete and felt that quitting was easier. She never
complained to me, she just quit. Period. Some Sweet
Sixteen.

Last month she came to me and told me she was
pregnant. She is going to keep the baby, and we are go-

ing to stand behind her. We will try and help her out the best we can. She has lost her self-esteem and I am going to try with all my might to help her re-find herself. I just pray to God that my husband finds a steady job before the baby is born. I don't blame welfare for my daughter's plight, but I feel that if things were just a little bit easier for us, maybe she would feel better about herself and things would have worked out differently.

I worry about my eight-year-old son. We live in a housing complex. There is an awful lot of drug use in our area. The kids he hangs out with are good kids, but they are all so easily led. I wish I had the extra money to get him more involved in sports; he played soccer for one season, but we couldn't afford another season. I pray to God that things will change in our lives before it's too late for him.

Our youngest daughter's biggest thrill of the week is Food Bank Wednesday. She goes with me and she usually gets free candy from them. I don't want her to get as frustrated as my other kids are. I hope things will change before she gets too much older.

I worry about the kids' teeth. We are not eligible for free medical or dental coverage. The medical is okay because we can purchase it privately, but not the dental. The kids haven't been to a dentist in over three years. My eldest daughter has had a cavity in her tooth for the last three years, my son needs dental work, and the youngest has never even seen a dentist. I had their names on a list at the university dental clinic, but when it came time for them to go (on two separate days), we just didn't have the money to get them there. My welfare worker told me of a place where we can get work done for a discounted price. The discount is 20% off, but on welfare there is no room for extras, even if it was 90% off. I pray that they can just hang on a little bit longer.

How can I define the feeling I have every night when

I go to bed? Some nights I just can't wait to go to bed. That's when I can finally take off that "happy face" and feel the way I really feel. No more putting on happy fronts for the kids or the neighbours, when all you really want to do is cry. Nighttimes are the worst for me. That's when all my thinking and worrying is done: "How will we get through another day? What will I feed them tomorrow? Who can I borrow from to make it just one more day? When will it end?" Usually through the sheer frustration of worry and crying I fall asleep, only to wake up to another day.

People never really think of what it's like to be poor until they are poor themselves. It's a sad fact but it's true. It doesn't help for someone to try it out for a day, or a month, or even six months. They have to live it. My husband is not one of those "welfare bums." He tries; he tries really hard. He doesn't like depending on the government to support us. If he could find a job today he would take it. But that is a pretty big "if" in this day and age.

There must be some way out of this nightmare. It's tough. It's really tough. We keep praying that tomorrow, maybe tomorrow, things will change, something will happen to make it a little easier until that job comes through. Someday...

O

In Canada, one of the richest countries in the world, more than half of the single mothers, almost 50% of unattached elderly and nearly one in five children are poor. They are among the 4.5 million Canadians living below the poverty line last year, 139,000 more than in 1991.

Vancouver Sun December 15, 1993

☐

Women face a significantly higher risk of poverty than men. Most of the differences between the sexes can be explained by the high poverty rates of three family types ... The 1993 poverty rate for unattached women under 65 was 37.9%, compared to 32.3% for unattached men under 65. For unattached seniors, the poverty rates were 47.3% for women and 32.1% for men. Single-parent families led by women with children under 18 had a poverty rate of 59.8% in 1993, a rate many times higher than the rates for married couples (12.4%).

Poverty Profile 1993
National Council of Welfare, Ottawa, 1995

☐

In 1993, 60% of poor families in Canada had incomes under the poverty line, even though the family head worked full time or part time during the year.

Figures from **Poverty Profile 1993**

☐

The authors of *The Canadian Fact Book on Poverty, 1989*
. . . find that the "market-income gap" (the gap that
would exist between the employment income of low
earners and the poverty lines if government transfers did
not exist to raise income) grew steadily and rapidly
between 1973 and 1986. The authors cite the inability of
employment growth to keep pace with new household
formation and low minimum wage levels as part of the
reason for the increase in the market-income gap.

Poverty in Canada by Helen McKenzie
Research Branch of the Library of Parliament
revised 18 March 1993

☐

In 1990, four out of five lone-parent families were headed
by women. Nearly half of these families had an income
of less than $20,000. There were 788,395 single-parent
families headed by women, with an average income of
$26,550. The average income for the 165,240 single-
parent families headed by men was $40,792.

Figures from **Family Income in Canada**
by Abdul Rashid (Focus on Canada Series)
Statistics Canada, 1994

☐

Photo: Pam Cooley

2.

Living on Welfare in B.C.: The GAIN Program

In British Columbia, income assistance is provided through a program called Guaranteed Available Income for Need (GAIN), which is administered by the Ministry of Social Services (MSS). The GAIN Act covers welfare, handicapped persons' allowance, low income earners' allowance and GAIN for seniors.

MSS divides people receiving GAIN into five categories: "employable," "unemployable," single parents, people with disabilities and people over age 65. The assistance rates are different for all five groups. People are considered "employable" if they have no physical or mental condition which keeps them from working, or if they are a couple, or two parents with children, and one adult has no physical or mental condition keeping him or her from working. Single parents with children under age 12 may be considered employable, but they may choose to stay home and look after their family.

Research done by the Social Planning and Research Council of B.C. (SPARC) has shown that GAIN rates would need to be raised anywhere from 45% to 75% to meet the average cost of basic living (including food, clothing, personal care, transportation and shelter, and excluding expenditures such as debt repayment, school equipment, health care expenses, insurance premiums, home maintenance and repairs, home equipment, and recreation or leisure) in the lower mainland of B.C. Although the percentages vary, GAIN rates fall far short of the average basic cost of living all across the province.

Additional allowances *may* be made to eligible GAIN recipients for the following: school start-up grants; Christmas supplement; daycare subsidy; special diet allowance; natal allowance, crisis grant; medical services plan. An earnings exemption of $100 a month for singles and $200 for families is allowed after three months. Employable recipients are also eligible for the Enhanced Earnings Exemption which allows an additional 25% exemption over the standard $100/$200 exemption.

Current GAIN rates are shown in the table on page 50. It should be noted that the shelter portion of GAIN includes utilities. Payment is made according to the recipient's actual rent and utilities costs, up to the maximum shown. (GAIN for handicapped people and for people over 65 is calculated using different rate schedules from the ones shown.)

In December 1989, there were 189,000 persons receiving basic income assistance in B.C. In December 1992, the number of recipients had increased by over 50% to 288,000 people.

Maintaining the Gap
October 1993

☐

In March 1994, 3,100,200 people in Canada depended on welfare. This was a 4.2% increase over the number in March 1993. There were 1,379,300 Ontario residents on welfare, 787,200 in Québec, and 353,500 in B.C.

Figures from **Health and Welfare Canada**

☐

GAIN Basic Assistance Rates (March 1994)

Rates for employable singles, couples, and 2-parent families where no family member is aged 60 to 64

Family Size	Support	Shelter Max.	Total Max.
1 person	$221	$325	$546
2 (couple)	$383	$520	$903
3 (couple with 1 child)	$486	$610	$1,096
4 (couple with 2 children)	$589	$650	$1,239
5 (couple with 3 children)	$692	$700	$1,392

Rates for unemployable singles, couples, and 2-parent families, or for people between age 60 and 64

Family size	Support	Shelter Max.	Total Max.
1 person	$271	$325	$596
2 (couple)	$433	$520	$953
3 (couple with 1 child)	$536	$610	$1,146
4 (couple with 2 children)	$639	$650	$1,289
5 (couple with 3 children)	$742	$700	$1,442

Rates for one-parent families

Family Size	Support	Shelter Max.	Total Max.
2 (parent with 1 child)	$462	$520	$982
3 (parent with 2 children)	$565	$610	$1,175
4 (parent with 3 children)	$668	$650	$1,318
5 (parent with 4 children)	$771	$700	$1,471

MONTHLY BUDGETS

DESCRIPTION: Single, employable woman, 25, living in a bachelor suite in Kitsilano

INCOME SOURCE: GAIN

	INCOME		EXPENDITURE		SURPLUS/ (DEFICIT)	SHORTFALL (percent)
BASIC SUPPORT	GAIN Support	$221.00	Food, Clothing, Personal Transport (SPARC estimate)	$455.77	($234.77)	52%
SHELTER	GAIN Maximum	$325.00	Rent/Utilities	$465.54	($140.54)	30%
TOTAL	**Maximum GAIN**	**$546.00**	**Support/Shelter**	**$921.31**	**($375.31)**	**41%**

INCOME SOURCE: Minimum wage

	INCOME		EXPENDITURE		SURPLUS/ (DEFICIT)	SHORTFALL (percent)
	Minimum Wage	**$1,040.00**	Expenditure	**$921.31**	**$118.69**	0

The shortfall column in these tables shows the difference between GAIN and estimated expenses as a percentage of expenses.

DESCRIPTION: One-parent family consisting of a mother, 26, and a son, 5, living in a 1-bedroom apartment in Marpole

INCOME SOURCE: GAIN

	INCOME		EXPENDITURE		SURPLUS/ DEFICIT	SHORTFALL (percent)
BASIC SUPPORT	GAIN Support	$462.00	Food, Clothing, Personal Transport (SPARC estimate)	$707.57	($245.57)	35%
SHELTER	GAIN Maximum	$520.00	Rent/Utilities	$684.26	($164.26)	24%
TOTAL	**Maximum GAIN**	**$982.00**	Support/Shelter	$1,391.83	**($409.83)**	**29%**

INCOME SOURCE: Minimum wage

INCOME		EXPENDITURE		SURPLUS/ DEFICIT	SHORTFALL (percent)
Minimum Wage	**$1040.00**	Expenditure	**$1,391.83**	**($351.83)**	25%

DESCRIPTION: One-parent family. Mother, 40, unemployable, with a son, 16, and a daughter, 14, living in a 3-bedroom apartment in New Westminster

INCOME SOURCE: GAIN

	INCOME		EXPENDITURE		SURPLUS/ (DEFICIT)	SHORTFALL (percent)
BASIC SUPPORT	GAIN Support	$565.00	Food, Clothing, Personal Transport (SPARC estimate)	$1,169.00	($604.00)	107%
SHELTER	GAIN Maximum	$610.00	Rent/Utilities	$764.26	($154.26)	25%
TOTAL	Maximum GAIN	**$1,175.00**	Support/Shelter	**$1,933.26**	**($758.26)**	**39%**

Information for these three tables is from *Maintaining the Gap*, Social Planning and Research Council of B.C. (SPARC), Vancouver, October 1993. The budgets have been updated using March 1994 GAIN rates.

MINIMUM WAGE RATES

B.C.	Alta.	Sask.	Man.	Ont.	Qué.	N.S.	N.B.	P.E.I.	Nfld.	Yukon	NWT
6.50	5.00	5.35	5.00	6.85	6.00	5.15	5.00	4.75	4.75	6.72	6.50

The National Council of Welfare has calculated that welfare rates across Canada fall anywhere from 24% to 80% below the poverty line.

Figures from **National Council of Welfare**

☐

In 1988, paid workers in Canada received an average of $29,969 in labour income. After adjusting for inflation, average income was actually 1.6% lower than 1977. Average labour income increased in the goods-producing sector but declined in the services-producing sector between 1977 and 1988.

Perspectives on Labour and Income Autumn 1990

☐

Single mothers are especially vulnerable to labour market poverty. For the majority of single mothers (57%), wages and salaries are their major income source. However, single mothers (21%) are less than half as likely as single fathers (52%) to earn more than $30,000 from wages, salaries, and self-employment.

Submission to the Ministerial Task Force on Social Security Reform
Canadian Advisory Council on the Status of Women (CACSW), March 1994

☐

POVERTY LINES IN CANADA

Family Size	Statistics Canada Low Income Cut-off for 1994		National Council of Welfare Low Income Cut-off: 1995 estimates		Canadian Council on Social Development Poverty Lines: 1994 estimates
	Rural $	City, 500,000 or more $	Rural $	City, 500,000 or more $	$
1	10,538	15,479	10,728	15,758	13,770
2	14,286	20,981	14,543	21,359	22,950
3	18,157	26,670	18,484	27,150	27,540
4	20,905	30,708	21,281	31,261	32,130
5	22,841	33,550	23,252	34,154	36,720
6	24,792	36,419	25,238	37,075	41,310
7	26,666	39,169	27,146	39,874	45,900

3.

Irene

Irene is a Native women in her late fifties. She lives on a welfare income, and is in poor health because of a severe beating.

It's the government's fault I am poor. I voted NDP, but the Socreds got in. I still go for NDP.

Poverty will change when women and kids come first. It wasn't from the government offering them that all us women got rights. I have two daughters; my son died when he was a year old. I've got beaten up but I try to stand up for my rights. Sometimes you got to help yourself.

O

Bessie

Bessie is a sixty-two-year-old white woman who was born in England. Her health is poor, and her income is from welfare.

My prison record keeps me poor, fourteen years in jail off and on. With a prison record like that, nobody wants to hire you. If society wouldn't be so damned prejudiced against us... The courses and training I got on the inside was no good on the outside.

I need a hearing aid, but welfare won't give me one; they say it's only for people who can get a job.

I think I will always be poor; it sure looks that way. No change year after year. No change; I see the same people all the time.

○

Patsy

Patsy is forty-nine. She is from Nova Scotia, has a Grade 10 education and lives on a GAIN income. Her health is poor.

Poverty is our nation's worst disease. It is incurable because of people's indifference. Nobody cares. If people cared, it would be different.

I have to go into the psych ward two or three times a year for a week. I am treated as if I am sick even when I am well. For me, the solution to poverty is suicide. I will be poor until I die. Nobody cares.

O

Cathy

Cathy is a twenty-nine-year-old white woman. Her income is from welfare. She has a Grade 11 education and has worked as a homemaker and a hostess.

I am poor because of an emotional disability; I am unable to work. I haven't had adequate help for this disability. I haven't got enough money to live.

I've been poor since I was seventeen. My own attitude has to change and so does that of society. My anger stops me from changing. There must be an end to class distinction. People need to work together instead of against each other. We need more facilities geared towards outreach, as there is not enough community outreach. Don't shut people away. The professionals are largely responsible for the unhealthy society we live in. Professionals and social workers put labels on people.

No, I won't always be poor. I think things are going to change.

○

Edith

Edith, forty-eight years old and living on unemployment in-
surance, was born in Scotland. She is a white woman with a
university education who is in good health.

I used to have good jobs, but they don't exist any
more. Sometimes I have to quit. I have never told a
boss that I have been on a psych ward, but they see the
scars on my wrist. Bosses are prejudiced against mental
sickness.

Poverty is part of the circle of isolation. Because I am
a woman alone, I will always be poor—unless I get a
rich man. Society punishes women who live on their
own. We are paid less than men; a woman alone is
poor.

We should change government priorities, more social
and human betterment. Food banks should not be
abolished. Society wants to make the poor invisible. We
have to make people more aware of poverty.

○

Donna

*Donna is a forty-one-year-old white woman who was born
in Quebec. She has a ninth-grade education. She is very sick,
and her only income is from GAIN.*

More and more is being taken away from me. Take,
take, take. I was a low-income worker but I had respect.
The respect is gone. I have not enough money for anything. Nothing to save. Identity is a problem. What am
I? Nobody understands.

If I had better health and could be logical about
things...if I had more money...if they mailed my
cheque...then I would perhaps feel respect for myself. I
don't want to be told where to live.

God forbid that I will always be poor. I cut my own
hair and do everything for myself. I am tired of living
around murderers and violence, tired of getting ripped
off.

O

Mabel

Mabel is a white woman with a middle-class background. She is forty-three years old. She was born in England, and is in fair health. She lives on welfare.

I have no faith in miracles, and fighting isn't my way. I don't go anywhere. I must go away; it's possible to get off Skid Row if you just get up and go.

There is no way that I will always be poor. I am poor because I got very sick. My illness is temporary—and if this is the worst that society can do to me, then it's not as bad as I feared.

O

Robbie

Robbie is a thirty-year-old woman. She has Grade 12 and one year of college.

I am poor because of self-worth problems. No, I won't always be poor. Welfare sucks!

O

Grace

Grace is a twenty-six-year-old white woman.

I am ill with agoraphobia. When my mate of five
years left in late March of 1985, I was virtually house-
bound. My feeling of self had diminished to almost
non-existence. I was able to travel about one mile away
from home in my car which was disintegrating rapidly,
making me even more anxious every time I had to go
out. I had not mingled with the public for several years
by this time and knew that there was no way that I
could hold a job away from my home. It was absolutely
impossible. I was left with no alternative but to turn to
the Ministry of Social Services and Housing for help.

The nearest Ministry office was four blocks away. I
went there armed with utility bills, rent receipts, personal data and information pertaining to my condition. I
slunk into the building before 8:30 and already people
were lined up, impatiently waiting for the door to open.
Mercifully, something inside me quelled my inner fears,
which told me to bolt and race home. I looked at the
gathering people curiously. They were of all ages, from
very young single mothers with runny-nosed pale children to men of close to retirement age dressed in worn-
looking suit jackets. Any eye contact was very brief. But
every face had one similar feature, and that was one of
hopelessness and frustration, which I will never forget
as long as I live. "My God," I thought, and later voiced
to a close friend who is agoraphobic too, "Will I look
like that too in a year's time or even less?"

My turn to be called for an interview took one and a

half hours. While I was waiting, I talked to a jeweller
and a construction worker for a short while. Both of
them had been out of work for eighteen months. Babies
squalled with boredom and mothers smiled sadly, apol-
ogetic.

The MSSH worker introduced herself and bustled me
into her office. I gave her my particulars in a shaky
voice, explaining why I could not work. My anxiety level peaked again, and her cold impersonal office intensi-
fied it.

She asked if I would go after my "ex" for support.
No, I would not; one of the reasons we split was financial. She pressed me to do it. I said, "Why create more
bad blood?" She dropped the subject.

I asked her about the possibility of getting a disability
pension, and she said that I could apply for one. What
she did not inform me was that, basically, according to
MSSH standards, a person must be bed-bound or in a
wheelchair to qualify for disability. She told me that I
would have to get a note from my physician saying that
I was unable to work because of agoraphobia. She
neglected to tell me that I stood a better chance of receiving unemployable status than disability, and that
even that would take eight months to begin coming in.

I asked her about schooling. I have my Grade 12 but
had taken a correspondence course through the Open
Learning Institute once. I told her that if I could get
funding for this type of schooling, which is in fact
cheaper than regular college, I could train myself in a
field where I could become self-sufficent. "You take
schooling," she replied, "and you won't get any
benefits." I could only stare at her. When she told me
that I would receive $350 per month, the tears started to
come. With great effort, I willed them back. My rent
was $365.

I left the office angry and desperate. I realized that
this system was designed to keep you well within their
control. It is unjust, demeaning, and bloody well harm-

ful to one's peace of mind. I thought back to those people in the corridor waiting, and wondered if I already
had that same look of hopelessness.

At home I was greeted by my cat, Gizmo. We sat together looking through the newspapers for a new place
to live. I was terrified. I knew that I needed security,
first of all. A place where I wouldn't be uprooted at any
given moment. The place had to be close to shopping,
for that was very important to my independence. Rents
for a one-bedroom apartment in my area run about
$300-$400 a month. Most of the city is about the same
price, with the exception of higher crime rate areas,
where a person who cannot afford insurance could easily become a victim and lose everything she has taken
years to acquire.

I had never given much thought to welfare, because
like most people, I never thought I would have to rely
on the system. I did know a few recipients and I called
them, realizing that they knew about the government's
regulations.

"What about moving into shared accomodation?" I
asked.

"Sure. Go ahead. What will you do with all your
stuff? Put it in storage? You can't afford that."

"What if I sold some of it?"

"If you sell anything, you have to declare it as income, then they knock that off your cheque. There's no
winning in losing."

What was I to do? My family was scattered throughout B.C., and were all dealing with their own personal
difficulties. I couldn't inflict my problems on them. Both
my parents are deceased, so I could not even turn to
them.

At the age of twenty-three, I began to feel much,
much older. My friends and family did help in any way
they could. Since I could not travel to the food bank because of my disability, friends would go for me. My
brother would come about twenty-five miles by bus,

bringing dinner as often as he was able. Other friends brought me cat food when they learned that I was thinking of giving my cat away, because they knew how important he was to me. Still others passed on their used clothing. I dropped from 145 to 117 pounds in two months. I made up the difference in my rent by getting an extra $35 a month collecting garbage and sweeping at the apartment complex where I live.

As the weeks went by I often had to sleep to ward off hunger pangs. I wrote a great deal about injustice and frustration. I also had for the first time in my life, because I was alone, a chance to study my inner self. I liked being on my own, even though it was a hard struggle and I was very frightened much of the time.

My MSSH caseworker started calling me about once every two weeks to see how I was managing. I detested these intrusions, since every time she phoned, visions of that first visit to the welfare office would depress me. She told me that I had to get a roommate. A roommate seemed logical, except that I only had one bedroom and I was enjoying my solitude and my own space. A couple of single mothers I knew had considered sharing a place with me, but the idea of disciplining children and the extra activity did not appeal to my overwrought nerves. My worker kept calling. I felt like I was being badgered, accused of surviving when I shouldn't have been. My stress level soared again at the idea of sharing my home and possessions with a complete stranger.

Finally, a friend told me of a mutual acquaintance who needed a place to stay. He was a nice young man who was never home except for meals and to sleep. I gave him the bedroom, myself the couch. I found that it was possible to share an apartment with a single man on a platonic basis. When he left, another friend needed to escape his environment and moved in. Having an apartment-mate did ease my financial burden.

My claim for unemployable status finally came through. I started to do telephone work as a volunteer for the B.C. Coalition of the Disabled; my task was to contact members and update their information. Some members talked at great length about their difficulties living on GAIN, and the way they felt humiliated by dependency on the government. Some were in the process of struggling to get a homemaker or fighting to get a disability pension. The word I kept hearing was "frustrated." How could a person ever get even a little bit ahead? All I could tell these people who were as confused and scared as I was was not to give up the most important thing of all—hope.

O

Poverty may be one of the greatest health hazards any society has ever faced.

The Unequal Society: A Challenge to Public Health   City of Toronto Department of Public Health, Toronto, November 1985

☐

Poverty kills more people in Canada than cancer.

Submission to the Ontario Social Assistance Review Committee Ontario Medical Association, January 9, 1987

☐

If you come from the lowest income group in Canada you can expect:
- an infant mortality rate
  1.95 times higher for male infants
  1.86 times higher for female infants
- an overall mortality rate
  1.48 times higher if you are male
  1.22 times higher if you are female
- a cardiovascular disease mortality rate
  1.33 times higher if you are male
  1.14 times higher if you are female
- a cancer mortality rate
  1.34 times higher if you are male
  1.07 times higher if you are female
- an accidents, poisoning and violence mortality rate
  1.88 times higher if you are male
  1.45 times higher if you are female

. . .

If you are from the lowest income group in Canada, you can expect to have:
- a prevalence of mental disorders
  2.09 times higher (both sexes)
- a prevalence of heart disease
  2.05 times higher (both sexes)

. . .

If you come from the lowest income group in Canada, you can expect:
- to live
  6.3 fewer years if you are male
  2.8 fewer years if you are female
- to be disability free
  14.3 fewer years if you are male
  7.6 fewer years if you are female
- to be unable to do your major activity
  7.6 more years if you are male
  1.5 more years if you are female
- to be restricted in your major activity
  2.2 more years if you are male
  4.6 more years if you are female
- to live a "quality-adjusted" (healthy) life
  10.3 fewer years if you are male
  5.1 fewer years if you are female

The Unequal Society 1985

☐

4.

Poverty and the Common Woman

Dorothy O'Connell

A version of this speech was given to an annual general meeting of the National Action Committee on the Status of Women in the late seventies.

I have a sign in my office that says: "I swear it to you, I swear on my common woman's head, The common woman is as common as a common loaf of bread...And will rise." I look at it whenever I get discouraged, and when I'm really discouraged, I chant it. I've been doing a lot of chanting lately.

It's a great sign. What's really great about it is that it says the *common* woman. ALL of us. Not just the exceptions, who chose the right field at the right time, but every single one of us will rise. Of course, when I'm really discouraged, I get really militant in my chanting, and when I'm not too discouraged, it's more of a calm certainty.

I'd be less militant if I really felt that all women want all women to rise. But of course, that's not true, unfortunately. A lot of women feel women should only rise if they've "earned" it. And who says what earning means? Those who've risen.

It is really too bad that all women don't share a common philosophy. There are very few feminists among poor women, and the reason for that is that the feminist movement, by playing up the right to work, and the right to leave the home, has downgraded even more those who don't choose to work, and the contempt for women in the home has grown, even among other women.

Poor women have always had to work, but it is not a choice. The kinds of jobs they get are strictly no-status jobs, with long hours, low pay, and terrible working conditions. When they get too old to work, they have varicose veins, or rheumatism, or asthma, or some other debilitating illness, and if they aren't old enough to get the government pension, they are allowed to apply for a disability pension which will keep them in one room on one meal a day. O brave new world!

And what about those women who stay home on welfare? Living in the lap of luxury on someone else's money, right? Yes indeed. "Why should I support you? I work hard for my money!" is a cry we often hear from men who are lawyers, or teachers. The assumption is that the woman on welfare is getting "something for nothing."

What is this nothing job she is doing for money somebody else earned? Raising her kids, for one thing. Well, of course, that's nothing. Driving a bus is important. Collecting garbage is important. But raising kids—any woman should be able to do that with one hand tied behind her back, right?

Of course, if you're on welfare, everybody in the world has the right to tell you you're not doing it right. How other women raise their children is a sacred subject. Strictly taboo for one woman to tell another how to raise her kids. Unless one woman is employed by the Board of Education or welfare or the Health Department or Children's Aid and the other is on welfare.

If each of her children does not have for breakfast two pieces of toast, one egg, one glass of orange juice, one bowl of cereal, and a glass of milk, the mother on welfare is going to hear about it. If a child goes to school in gumboots because she has no running shoes, Mother is going to hear about it. If a child misses school because there is no money for winter boots, Mother is going to hear about it.

She's going to hear about the Canada Food Rules. She's going to hear about taking proper care of her young. What she is not going to hear is an incredulous voice saying: "You get *how* much money to live on? How do you do it?" She's going to hear a little lecture on proper budgeting from a young single woman earning a measly wage of $20,000 and unable to save enough money for the things she really wants.

And how much money is the woman on welfare raising kids living on? Less than half the poverty level. Her welfare money is divided into two parts—shelter and support. If she's not lucky enough to live in public housing or a co-op, the rest of the rent has to come from the support portion, which is for food, clothing, transportation, recreation, Hydro, telephone, and so on.

An interesting sidelight, by the way, is that this money is not a right. The family allowance is every woman's. But not welfare. That's a loan. Payable any time you have money. If you win $500 at bingo, they take it. If you get insurance money, they take it. If your husband pays child support, they take it. And if they catch you committing fraud, you lose the whole bundle. Fraud can be an estranged husband staying overnight a few times, or a boyfriend, even if they can't prove he contributed a penny; or (horrors) it can be working and not reporting the money. A case in Toronto involved a woman with six kids on Family Benefits [Ontario welfare program for families on long-term assistance] who earned $3,000 a year driving a school bus. She was thrown in jail for four months, as an example. $3,000 a year added to her Family Benefits wouldn't bring her up to the poverty line. No mention was made of whether her rent was exorbitant, whether she was being gouged for money by all and sundry, just her crime. A few years ago, 9,000 people committed fraud. They answered incorrectly a form which asked them if they had ever owned their own home before. They included a Conservative MP and a Liberal who worked for Prime Minister Trudeau. It was decided that the question was too hard, and had been misunderstood. Nobody went to jail. As far as I know, they didn't even have to pay back the money. $9 million and nobody went to jail.

Poverty is blamed on the poor, in this country. They must deserve it. If they're immigrant women the answer is, "Well, if they don't like it, they can always go back where they came from." If they are Native women: "Well, you know what Indians are like. Those people have no work ethic." If they are single women: "Let them get married." A couple of years ago, *Chatelaine* ran an article called "How I Got Out of Public Housing." First, the welfare recipient told all about how she hated being on welfare and living in public housing. Then she told all about her marvellous Family Benefits worker, who got her back into school. The story ended when she met a man in a bar and married him. One presumes she lived happily ever after, in their trailer, with four children. What a success story!

What about leaving welfare, if it's so bad, and going to work? Well, there's no work; there's no daycare. And if by some miracle you get work and daycare, how long do you suppose this lasts? Last year, our organization hired a woman who was on Family Benefits. First, her worker told her that she would be entitled to phase-out money. Then she got a letter which said, "Sorry, but the work is temporary. On a grant. You can't have phase-out money." Then she was told she could stay on Family Benefits for $2.50 a month, so that at least her medical care and dental care for her children would be covered. Then she got a letter from the Ontario Housing Authority: "Because you are now working, your rent is going up." At the end of six months, when the grant was over, and she needed to reapply for Family Benefits, she got a letter which said, "Sorry. We miscalculated. You owe $126." She appealed. She won. But during an appeal, you can't collect Family Benefits. The appeal took months. In the meantime, she lived on emergency welfare. The day she got out of the hospital from having a tubal ligation, so she wouldn't have any more children, she had to take a bus to the other end of town to pick up her food money, because it wasn't their policy to mail it. Teach her to work, eh?

Later, we hired two women on welfare. We thought we'd be smarter. We got the work called a training program, so they could keep their $2.50 per month. It looked simple. The first woman arranged for daycare. This took some time, and entailed leaving work, taking a bus to the other end of town, and waiting an hour or two to sign forms. Finally it was done. Then she had to leave work to go to welfare and sign forms. This was also at the other end of town. Then, unexpectedly, a transfer came through. She could have a house for herself and her two small children, instead of an apartment in a high-rise. But only if she moved the following Monday. Then, she had to rearrange daycare, because it was at the other end of town. She had to switch her children to separate school, because they took four-year-olds all day. Then she had to have an operation. When she came back to work, she got a phone call from daycare telling her that she couldn't work Mondays. No daycare. She fought. Then they phoned her and said, "All set. But you can't work Thursdays." Then she got a letter from the school saying that although her son had lots of friends, he was not a sociable child, and they recommended that she take him one afternoon a week to a psychiatrist. Then the psychiatrist told her she seemed hostile. Does this seem unlikely?

What is interesting is how many of these people doing this to her were other women. Everyone but the psychiatrist. Our other employee is still trying to get permanent daycare. Why don't these women work if they don't like welfare?

Welfare is slavery. It is life imprisonment for the whole family. Shortly it may be starvation. Sounds dramatic, eh? Maybe a little over-emotional. Let's talk about it. Maybe it will go away.

Women are being forced to go to churches and beg for food vouchers. A food voucher from a church averages $15. Can't get much food for $15. So they hit several churches. What is the church reaction? Is it "Good heavens! There must be real poverty in this country?" No, it's "Watch out!

There's a lot of fraud. These families are playing the system. Don't give them any food vouchers."

We may shortly be in a position where flu may kill our babies, where diarrhea may kill our babies. Infant mortality will go up. There's already screaming by the government about not having enough children to fill the schools we've built. Who is going to have these children? More and more middle-class women are saying, "Not me! I have a career! I choose not to have children." So if you people don't have them, and ours die, how do we keep the country going? Keep importing immigrant women to do the housework?

Once upon a time, the poor ate well. That's when brown rice was cheap, brown sugar was cheap, unrefined anything was cheap. But health foods became a fad, and now the stuff that's cheap isn't good for you.

Who are the women we are talking about, anyway? The poor have always been with us, right? The ones who have a Grade 4 education, and who quit school to become hairdressers?

Some of us are. But others, more and more others, are simply the victims of marriage break-up. Middle-class women, who went to school as far as high school, or even to university. They got married to someone who left them, or who inconsiderately died, or went crazy, or went to jail, or got fired, or beat them. Or they are women who worked until they had a nervous breakdown, or they have epilepsy, or diabetes.

Any woman can be deprived of any money at any time, if she is not independently wealthy. Oh, under the new family laws, if you worked and contributed money to the home, you're entitled to half. But if all you did was keep the home fires burning, you can forget a pension or half the property. But listen, you can keep the kids. Usually.

If you've stayed home, raising the kids, because you thought you should, and your husband decides he prefers a younger woman, who is going to hire you when you hit forty? Oh, they're not allowed to discriminate because of age—but if you're not pretty, there are all kinds of jobs you can't get, serving the public.

Well, what has all this got to do with you? Sad, isn't it? Touching? But maybe not very relevant?

Well, what it's got to do with you is: first, you may not believe it, but it could happen to you. Or your daughter. Secondly, no woman is an island. We are the women who take care of your kids, who clean your houses, so you can go to work. Third, if welfare rates go up, so does the minimum wage, which will help other women.

The feds will tell you that welfare is a provincial responsibility, and the province will tell you that they only get so much money from the feds for social services, and it's being cut back, so what can they do?

Women and children in need are everybody's responsibility. So is the issue of food prices. Lobby for more money for social services. Ask for more subsidies. Ask for an investigation of a food industry whose profits are enormous. Ask for more jobs for women. Keep up the attack on slashes in unemployment benefits, in training allowances. But remember us, your sisters, when you ask for bigger salary increases for women in your field.

And ask us to join you, to speak with you—don't shut us out. This is not just Pierre Berton's Canada, or Pierre Trudeau's—it belongs to every one of us who typed a line, or raised a child, or swept a floor, or planted a garden. We helped settle this land—some of us a hundred years ago, some of us a thousand years ago, some of us yesterday. But we belong here. We *work* here, no matter what it is we do. And we're not going to go away, or be quiet, or be respectful, or be grateful. We're here to stay, and we want justice! Don't give us your old clothes. Give us your support.

Dorothy O'Connell is an Ottawa writer and long-time poverty rights activist. She is the author of three books: Chiclet Gomez *(Deneau & Greenberg, 1977),* Cockeyed Optimist *(Deneau, 1980) and* Sister Goose *(Steel Rail, 1987).*

O

5.

Jackie

Jackie has completed two years of college. She is a white woman, thirty-eight years of age. She has worked in the social services.

It's simple—I am poor because I'm unemployed. Employment at a decent wage would be a solution to my poverty. I think one day I will be middle-income. Government should fund social services at the community level.

O

Tracy

Tracy has a Grade 12 education, and has worked as a waitress, done reception work, and been a stripper and a hooker. She is a white woman of twenty-one in good health. Her income is from GAIN.

I am poor because there are no real jobs. My age has been a problem with jobs; nobody wants to give you a chance. People with jobs assume that anybody can get a job. People like social workers and welfare workers treat you like a dummy. They don't really give a shit. I think I will always be poor.

O

Sybil

Sybil is a Native woman in her sixties. She lives on a handicapped pension.

I am poor because I was brought up poor, with no education except how to look after my mother's babies, and housework. I do think that when you are young you should learn sewing, cooking, and get as much education as you can. My mother told me, "You don't need an education—your husband will take care of you." She wanted to pick a husband for me. Poverty can be a pattern your mother gets you into.

Another $25 a week would make a difference to me. But the only way I wouldn't be poor is if I found another Jim Pattison!

O

Doreen

Doreen is a white woman of fifty-five whose income is from a handicapped pension. She has one year of college and a certificate for social service work, and she has done community work for many years.

I am poor because the kind of work I do well, which is community work, doesn't have a salary now as it did in the past. I supported my family as a single mother. Now I am a poor older woman. My children are grown, and it should be a good time financially for me, but it's not.

If my skills and my worth were judged by the community, I would be employed and not poor. I am discriminated against because of my age.

I am not sure if I will always be poor. It looks that way. If I can only hang on to my self-esteem and feelings of self-worth—being on assistance gives one a negative feeling towards oneself.

○

Gus

Gus is a thirty-four-year-old white woman. Her health is good. She has a welfare income.

I am poor because there are no decent jobs available. I don't have the skills. I have a university education, but I'm overeducated and underskilled. I also have a learning disability, and I'm poor because of society's attitudes towards mental illness, depression, and obvious gaps in my work history.

If only there could be meaningful job training, not just for cheap labour. Assets should be developed. People should be allowed to do the best with what they have got.

Welfare is not adequate, and you can't get off it. I have no hope. I have no job. I have no job opportunities. People like me do not get a chance.

○

Tina

Tina is a young woman eighteen years of age. She is angry and frustrated with her work situation.

Why am I poor? Because my job doesn't pay me enough to live on. I work at McDonald's, but it's always part-time. I never make full-time, so I don't get any benefits or job security.

When I went to school I quit in Grade 9. I went to work, but after the summer I was laid off. I would like employers to be made to be more responsible, and not be allowed to use workers, then throw them away like garbage.

I would like to have a full-time job. I have to make my room rent. I don't want welfare. Sometimes I think about becoming a hooker. I think working for companies that keep your hours down makes a woman look for a man to help her. I've got a boyfriend. He helps with the rent. He pushes me around when he's high. He really beat me up last Christmas. If I had a good job with a pay that I could live on, maybe I could leave him. I don't know. Maybe I'll go back to school.

If I could change things I would make it easier to go back to school. I would make these outfits pay a wage that people could live on. I would give every poor person a dentist and medicine. My teeth are bad! I would make bus fare cheaper. It costs so much to go to work. Like, if I only get four hours work and I have to pay bus fare, it's hard. I'd make rich people have to give some of their money to the poor.

O

Angela

Angela is a single mom. She is thirty-two. She has a high school education.

I am poor because I work for minimum wage in a factory. I also work weekends. My mom takes care of my daughter. I don't pay her very much. I chip in for the groceries, though, about $35 a week.

I've got an old car. I need it to get to work, but the gas and insurance keeps me broke. But I'm going to keep it. It's all I've got for working so hard.

I keep away from welfare. I was in some trouble when I was younger and when my kid was six months old, they were going to take her away from me, so I don't want anything to do with welfare. I'll work three jobs to keep us together if I have to.

I think I'm poor because I have no real skills. I would like to be a carpenter. I always liked wood—the smell of it, the creative feeling of making something. Even as a little kid, I loved to hammer and make stuff out of old wood that I found in the alley. Girls are not supposed to like that stuff, though.

I like a few beers after work. I put my kid to bed, I turn on the TV, I drink a few beers. I have to have some pleasure.

Will I always be poor? I won't be rich, that's for sure. Things would change if I could learn a profession, if rents were cheaper and gas was cheaper and food was cheaper. How come I always have to give up the little I earn to make Safeway and the gas companies richer? Maybe I'll find a man with money. Maybe I'll win the Lotto. Maybe I'll get sick and die; then it won't matter.

O

In 1992, women employed full-time, full-year earned just
72% the figure for their male counterparts. This,
however, was up from 68% in 1990 and around 64% in
the early 1980s.

Women in the Labour Force 1994
Statistics Canada, October 1994

☐

Most women continue to work in traditionally female-
dominated fields. In 1991, 71% of women were employed
in just five occupational groups—teaching (6%), nursing
or related health occupations (9%), clerical (29%), sales
(10%), and service (17%). In contrast, only about 30% of
employed men worked in one of these occupational
groupings.

"Women in the Workplace"
by Nancy Zukewich Ghalam
in *Canadian Social Trends*
Spring 1993

☐

Employed women are less likely than men to be covered
by a pension plan—39% compared to 50%. Just 62% of
women aged 15 to 64 contributed to the Canadian or
Québec Pension Plan, versus 80% of men.

Women in the Workplace 2nd edition
by Nancy Zukewich Ghalam
Statistics Canada, March 1993

☐

Minimum wages are not enough to escape poverty. The
earnings of one person with a full-time minimum-wage
job are below the poverty line in most Canadian cities.
Even the earnings of two full-time minimum-wage jobs
do not bring a family of four above the poverty line in
these same cities.

Fact Sheet on Women and Poverty
CACSW, November 1991

□

Since 1975, federal, provincial, and territorial governments in Canada have allowed the real value of minimum
wages to erode by 20% to 30% through a policy of
neglecting to raise them in accordance with rises in
average industrial wages

. . .

The proportion of women working at or below the
minimum wage rate is significantly higher than the
proportion of men. Low minimum wages clearly create
disincentives to work. In 1992, a full-time minimum-
wage job under federal jurisdiction yielded a gross
income of 55% of the poverty line. Minimum-wage jobs
currently yield gross incomes below the poverty line in
every province and territory in Canada.

Submission to the Ministerial Task Force
on Social Security Reform
CACSW, March 1994

□

Daphne

Daphne is a white woman in her mid-thirties.

Why am I poor? That's an easy question to answer. I work for minimum wage and I can't save any money. I was turned down for a student loan. I have no way of buying medicine when I'm sick—I needed antibiotics but I had no money so I didn't get them.

What can be done? Free education. Free medicine. A much higher minimum wage. Make society realize that every human being is important and should be loved and cared for and nurtured. In our present society, everybody just climbs on top of each other, crushing the person below them.

Will I always be poor? I think I will be poor, but when I'm dead it won't matter, because you sure as hell can't take it with you. So rich and poor will be equal in death.

O

Micheline

Micheline is a thirty-four-year-old white woman who was born in Quebec. She is in good health, and she has two years of university education and many work skills.

I would be poor whether I worked a forty-hour week or not. When I worked, I was making only slightly more than assistance. This was because I chose to work with women and children. I also pursued my art career. Poetry doesn't pay the rent.

I would like to see wages for volunteer work. I'm sure I will always be poor.

○

Helga

Helga is a white woman fifty-seven years of age.

I've been working for Statistics Canada for two and a half years. In the last four years or so, nobody has been hired as a permanent worker. There is no union, we are not protected. You're not a civil servant because you're under the Statistics Act. We don't get medical coverage, and we get vacation pay on every cheque, 4% every two weeks. So you get this 4%, and you can never take a holiday because you don't get a cheque if you take a holiday.

Our hours can be cut down to the point where you can't live on your wages, so you leave. Somebody asked for a holiday about three weeks ago—she had to go to a wedding—and they said that she couldn't have it. They said, "Well, that's fine, if you want to go away then we'll hire somebody else and then we'll have fewer hours a month for *everybody* in September." That's how they threaten you. They started here in Vancouver to get us into a union, but nothing's been done. We are too small a group. We're only a drop in the bucket.

You don't get pension, you don't get nothing. Like when I have to stop work, all I'll have is my unemployment for a year.

Everybody is doing that, everybody that can get away with it. I mean, Safeway does it, lots of companies do. You know, even United Cigar does it. The girls only work thirty hours a week, part-time. It is the new trend. It's okay if you have a husband who supports you and you just need a little bit of extra money and you have a couple of days to kill. I mean, I wouldn't mind being on five or ten days a month and having some pocket money. Then I would have the rest of the time to do things for myself. But if you're the sole supporter, you have to pay your bills and you can't do it.

I live in B.C. Housing. Rent used to be 25% of your income. Now it is 30%. If you have a son or daughter who lives with you and makes some money, even if they're teenagers, you have to pay 30% of their income too. So you can't win. Plus you have to pay for your own cable, your own Hydro, plus you have to pay $5.00 for gas for some crazy reason.

You know, you are better off on welfare, I don't care what anybody says. Because you can always do some babysitting, cleaning houses; you can always do something extra, you know. But not everybody is cut out for that kind of thing. I don't like doing my own housework, why should I go and clean somebody else's house?

I was on welfare until two and a half years ago. I had to do it, because I had children and I didn't feel it was right because, when I'm working, by the time I get home at night I am just exhausted, I am like a vegetable most of the time. How can you look after kids, make sure they do their homework, make sure their clothes are clean and everything else?

My kids never knew I was on welfare. I always worked part-time, and then I reported that income and I got the rest of my income from welfare. The kids thought I was making it all the way. I never told them. Now they know. At the time, I had five kids at home and I was the sole supporter so they knew it was hard. You know, even if I hadn't been on welfare, it would have been hard. In thinking back, it seems now almost impossible. But if you have to do something, you can do it. I don't care who you are. Unless you drink or smoke a lot. You couldn't make it if you smoked or drank.

Not that I want to go back on welfare, but you are better off financially. I'm a diabetic. On welfare, my insulin was paid for, my medical coverage was paid for. Now I have to pay every cent. But I prefer to work. You know, when you sit at home and you haven't got your bills paid, when the phone rings you are afraid to pick it up, you are afraid it is a bill collector. If the doorbell rings, you're afraid you're behind with something, or when you're late paying, you're afraid your phone is cut off. At least if you go to work, you go, you come home and nobody really bothers you at night. And that's different. It's more nerve-wracking when you owe money to be home than to be out working. And when you're tired and you feel like quitting, well, you talk yourself out of it. I don't like the work itself, but I like the people I'm working with. There's insecurity with my job, but you're insecure on welfare too. But you know, people who have never done without, they don't realize what it's like.

I guess I was brought up to work but I wouldn't advise anybody else to do it. If people say, well, I'd rather stay on welfare, that's their privilege. Everybody has to make up their own mind. It's not easy on welfare, but it's not easy in the work force either. When you're working, you have to have the clothes. If you are home, you can have two or three good dresses or whatever. You don't have to have pantyhose in the winter, you don't have to dress up the same way.

I think things are going to change for the worse instead of the better. I mean, I see it all around me. So many companies are starting to do the same thing as the government, hiring people part-time. And there is such unemployment that people either work part-time or not at all.

Canada is governed by maybe ten families at the most and they have the money and they pull the strings and we are the puppets. And unless they try to make things better, I don't see any hope. I really don't. They're the ones who have the wealth and they bribe the politicians, they bribe the police, they bribe everything.

I have no faith in the system. I would love to see the NDP come in and I only hope that they don't end up being typical politicians getting bribed too. Maybe there is a bit of hope if the NDP come in and we have good people like Margaret Mitchell [NDP Member of Parliament for Vancouver East], I think she has a handle on it. But I don't know if she is strong enough. Now Broadbent is in a popular position, and he already has started waffling a little bit. Saying maybe privatizing is a good idea and all this kind of stuff. And he is not even in, he is just good in the polls. And this free market they are talking about would hinder us.

I think I'll always be poor. I've lived with it so far, I can live with it. I mean, I'm not expecting anything spectacular. But I feel sorry when I see people with young children.

You hear them talk on TV. There's a group now who wants to get more security for people who get laid off between fifty and sixty-five who can't find a job anymore and who are alone. They are aware of it, the government, but they don't do anything. I don't want to be pessimistic but I don't see anything happening; I really don't.

O

Most part-time jobs (72%) are held by women, partly
because women still carry the main burden of domestic
responsibilities and partly because jobs in the retail and
service sectors, where women predominate, are likely to
be part-time jobs. Many of these jobs pay lower wages
than full-time jobs, and they lack benefits such as paid
holidays, pensions and job security. They also offer little
or no union protection, training or promotion.

Women, Poverty and Public Policy 1985

☐

Even when they are employed, women still maintain
primary responsibility for household work. In 1986,
employed women spent 3.2 hours per day performing
unpaid household tasks, versus 1.8 hours for comparable
men.

Women in the Workplace

☐

In 1994, 26% of all women employed outside the home
worked part-time. This compared with just 10% of
employed men. Women accounted for 69% of all
part-time employees in Canada in 1993. Over 500,000
women, 34% of female part-time workers, wanted but
could not find full-time employment. The latter figure
was up from 20% in 1989.

Women in the Labour Force 1994

☐

Only 43% of employment losses incurred in 1991 and 1992 were recovered [in 1993] . . . Nearly 60% of the total growth in employment in 1993 consisted of part-time work and almost three-quarters of these 85,000 additional part-time workers were adults.

"The labour market: Year-end review" by Cécile Dumas in *Perspectives on Labour and Income*, Spring 1994

☐

Almost half (46%) the increase of 3.5 million jobs between 1975 and 1993 came from part-time jobs, so that by 1993 nearly one-quarter of all jobs provided less than 30 hours of work per week. [Part-time jobs accounted for 23% of all jobs in 1993, compared with only 14% in 1975.]

"Jobs! Jobs! Jobs!" by Henry Pold in *Perspectives on Labour and Income*, Autumn 1994

☐

A September 1992 social report for Metropolitan Toronto revealed one in five workers there with only part-time employment. Families whose heads work part-time are five times more likely to be poor than those whose heads are full-time workers. Similarly, nearly half of unattached individuals who work part-time are under the poverty line as compared to only 8.7% of unattached full-time workers. Part-time workers tend to be paid less and fringe benefits such as pensions and insurance coverage are often not extended to them.

Poverty in Canada

☐

6.

Working as a Welfare Advocate

Sheila Baxter

From 1984 to 1987, I worked as a volunteer welfare advocate in Vancouver's Downtown Eastside. People often asked me, what does a welfare advocate do? As an advocate, I provided welfare advice, and also stood by people when they had been unjustly treated, giving them all the support I possibly could to rectify the situation. For me, an important part of advocacy is treating people as equals, as friends travelling along the same road.

The stories that follow are typical of the kinds of problems women on welfare face, and the kinds of things an advocate can sometimes do to help them. Some of these stories don't have a happy ending; some don't have an ending at all, because the women came to see me once or twice and then disappeared from the community. I never knew if they had died or been institutionalized or just moved on. And in some cases, the women I talked to were already too demoralized to go through the steps necessary to appeal an unjust Ministry of Social Services and Housing decision, so I was able to give support and advice, but not to take the matter any further.

There are welfare advocates in the downtown areas and in the suburbs. They often consult with one another, sharing a kind of network of knowledge. Many of the people I worked alongside belong to End Legislated Poverty, a coalition of anti-poverty groups around B.C. To find a welfare advocate in your area, contact one of the anti-poverty groups listed in the back of this book.

. . .

We sat talking together, two women having a coffee at the local community centre. Ashley was a tiny woman, about twenty-six. She had a little two-year-old with her. She looked pale and tense; her eyes were a reflection of the struggles she was going through. Ashley's other child, a four-year-old who had been deaf for a year, was in pre-school. He had had an operation, and his hearing was fine now, but he still had speech problems. He had a lot of catching up to do.

I asked her if she had a bus pass. She said no, her worker wouldn't give her one, so she walked to the centre and home, making four trips a day. She was determined to keep her kid in pre-school. We talked about welfare and how hard it was to manage on such little money. Ashley was scared. She was taking care of a friend's baby four nights a week. She couldn't take cash because she would have to declare it to welfare, so her friend bought groceries once a week for her.

Ashley said, "I feel like a thief. I feel like I'm doing something real bad, but I have to feed my kids. I know it's dishonest, and I worry, what if they find out? I'm so tired of the struggle. The doctor said I'm anaemic; that's why I'm so tired. I'm going to have to eat better. It's awful to feel that you are frauding, yet I work hard for those groceries. That baby is really active."

I told her she could appeal the bus pass. She said, "No, I don't want to make *them* mad at me."

. . .

Marianne is a single mom who really tries hard to manage on welfare. She shops in thrift stores, buys day-old bread, and goes to the food banks, lining up in the rain for a couple of hours to get a ticket and then going back for the food. Marianne does a few hours of community work each week, too, and has to pay her own bus fare. When she came to see me, she was shaking and crying. She said, "This is the last straw. I can't take any more."

Marianne was happy that welfare had paid for her kids to go to summer day camp. It was quite far from her house, and the kids bussed it every day. This had been authorized by a summer replacement worker at the welfare office. Now, in October, her regular worker at welfare was saying, "The replacement worker had no right to allow bus fare for summer day camp. You have to pay it back." So money was being deducted each month from her meagre food allowance to repay this.

I was really angry at the stupidity of this. I talked to Marianne's worker, who was quite serious about repayment. In fact, I found her to be totally uncaring, unsympathetic, and not open to reason. I then talked to a supervisor who was more understanding, and she called me back to say that the bus fare would not be stopped out of this mom's cheque.

For Marianne, this incident wasn't just a question of money. It was the powerlessness she felt, the low self-esteem that happens when welfare has so much power over your life. This mom and her kids are human beings with feelings and needs. How can the system treat them like a set of books to be balanced?

. . .

Jay is the mother of two children. She is thirty-two years old. She came to me upset and fed up. She had a job that she liked at $4.00 an hour, and MSSH was giving her a subsidy to bring her wages up to welfare level. Welfare paid for her kids to be in daycare, but she needed a bus pass to get to the daycare centre and to work. She was refused. She had to quit work because she couldn't afford the bus fare to take her kids to daycare and go to work herself.

I asked Jay's worker why Jay couldn't get a bus pass. Answer: "The pass is provided if the kids are in daycare only if Jay has mental or physical problems." Because this woman is fighting to work and to stay well, she cannot have a bus pass! If she becomes emotionally sick or has "problems," then she is eligible.

Unfortunately, the line workers in welfare offices have to follow these absurd policy regulations. Jay could have gone the appeal route, but she said, "To hell with them. I'm tired of fighting to survive."

. . .

June is a single mother of two kids. She wanted to do some meaningful community volunteer work. But it costs money to volunteer, as all volunteers know. June couldn't afford the bus fare because her welfare cheque is so little and bus fares are expensive.

She was refused a bus pass because she is not sick. If, however, she becomes emotionally ill, goes to therapy or A.A. meetings or makes frequent psychiatric visits, she will probably be able to get bus fare from welfare. The message is loud and clear—get sick, develop emotional problems, and you will get help and a little more money. But the big problem *then* is that your kids could finish up in foster care.

I suggested that June appeal this, but she declined, saying, "Forget it. What's the use of trying?"

. . .

Adella is a single mother. She had recently started her four-year-old son in pre-school, and welfare was giving her coupons to pay for this. At first, she was really happy with the arrangement. But then she realized she couldn't afford to have her son in the pre-school program, even with the subsidy.

She told me, "I'm going to have to take him out of that school. Welfare won't give me the bus fare to take him there and back. I tried, but paying out the $2.50 for bus fare leaves me so broke; I couldn't buy milk this morning. We can't walk it—it's thirty-five blocks each way. My welfare worker told me to take the money out of my food budget, but there's not enough."

Adella had tears in her eyes and I could feel her frustration and anger. I told her she could appeal by speaking to the supervisor at her welfare office, but she turned a sad face towards me and said, "Forget it."

. . .

A group of women were sitting around the women's centre discussing welfare. Most of them lived in downtown hotel rooms because that was all their shelter allowance from welfare—$250 a month—would allow.

Fatima said, "Hey, guess what? My worker gave me a bus pass!" She wore a big smile, and wasn't showing signs of depression as she had last week. "I can go to my A.A. meetings. I can go to thrift stores all over the place. I went out of the city on Saturday, and saw a cheap place to rent. It's so great having a bus pass. I don't have to stay downtown."

Celestine: "Why the hell won't my worker give me one? I've got the same problems you have. I asked her, and she said no. What a bitch she is. Why can't I have a bus pass? It's not fair."

As the women all know, some welfare workers are really great and will listen and help as much as they possibly can within their policy restrictions, but others just use their authority to have power over women. We talked about a woman's right to appeal workers' decisions, but Celestine felt it would just make her worker treat her worse. She and the others were scared that if they appealed or complained, their cheques would be cut. This can't happen, of course, but a worker certainly has the power to make a woman's life happier—or more miserable. And then there are the supervisors who squash the front-line workers, and all the other bosses at various levels who shove their employees around. Office politics could be the only reason Celestine hasn't got a free bus pass.

. . .

Corinne was having a difficult time. Her unemployment insurance had run out, and she was back on welfare again. She had been on it before, and hated it. "You know, I hate having a woman worker. It's like she is your peer, but looking down on you if you don't subdue yourself. She gives you a hard time. I like a man worker; I know how to handle them. I know what to say. I know how to tell them what they want to hear, and usually I get treated well."

. . .

Flora's whole body shook. "I hate him, the bastard. I hate him, but they won't let me change workers. Why can't I have a woman, a woman who would understand me and I could talk to her? I hate him. He had my kid apprehended. I hate him. Do you hear me? I hate him."

. . .

I met Dee a year ago. She had a hyperactive four-year-old daughter who had been kicked out of various daycares. Dee was living in a small, cramped suite. She had tried to work at a cashier's job to support herself and her daughter, but just couldn't handle it. The money wasn't enough and nobody seemed to understand the stress of coping with a daughter who had really special needs. Dee gave up and just let everything go. All she did was cry. Her MSSH worker at the time seemed to blame her. The child was close to being apprehended.

Recently, I ran into Dee on the bus. She looked happy, and her daughter sat contentedly beside her, looking out the window. We talked for a few minutes. Dee had a new welfare worker, and her life had changed dramatically.

"Guess what? I'm going to school this summer, and in September I start a nursing course. I have a five-year plan. I don't want just a certificate, I want a degree.

"I'm living in a two-bedroom apartment in a real neat co-op. Can you believe it? I have my own space, and so does my daughter. It's subsidized; it's great. My new worker has really encouraged me. I have a bus pass to go to school. Daycare for Allison is a latchkey program for the summer, then they'll take her to kindergarten for me. I'm getting so much help from my worker. She likes me."

She turned to me with a smile as she got off the bus. "I'll invite you to my grad a few years from now."

. . .

Trixie came to see me about a deduction in her welfare cheque.

"All I have ever been, as far as work goes, is an exotic dancer and a hooker. I lived in thirty-eight foster homes and two institutions while I was growing up. I'm thirty. I just got my kid back from welfare. They won't get him again.

"I was beat up real bad by a john, almost killed. He tried to murder me. Welfare said my son was at risk, but now I've got him back and those jerks won't get him again. He's my son and I love him.

"To keep my son, I've gotta stay out of hooking. But how the hell am I supposed to pay the rent on my welfare money? It's $500 a month for my two-bedroom. I've lived there for six years and I don't want to move. Anyway, you can't get a two-bedroom for much less.

"They've taken $100 off my welfare cheque this month. You know, they are forcing me back onto the streets. They leave me no choice—I don't want to turn tricks again, but how are we going to eat?"

I placed a call to the welfare office. "Hello, is this Ms. B? I am the advocate for Trixie K. There is a deduction to her cheque. Could you please explain why?"

Ms. B: "If she wants to know why, she must make an appointment to see me next week. Tell her to bring her rent receipt."

Me: "She doesn't have enough money to pay her rent."

Ms. B.: "The first time I have available is next Tuesday."

Me: "But that's six days away. We just want to know the exact reason for the deduction so that we can appeal it."

Ms. B: "I'm sure that won't be necessary. I think Trixie has problems that she hasn't discussed with you. She is upset about something else."

Trixie: "She's such a bitch! Such a bitch! I hate her forcing me back on the streets!"

At this point, a fairy godmother waves a wand, and good jobs and real training and free education appear. Trixie is given a good dose of high self-esteem. The thirty-eight foster homes are erased from her memory, and all the abusive johns are jailed. Trixie and her son live happily ever after.

But there is no magic, only the reality of not enough money to pay the rent, and no way to bottle high self-esteem, and johns don't get jailed very often.

. . .

The welfare system in every province in Canada is a complex operation governed by a vast array of rules which require interpretation and the exercise of administrative discretion. Personal judgements invariably give rise to inconsistencies in the treatment of recipients within and between jurisdictions. The fact that the rules are neither well known nor well understood by the public makes it difficult to verify whether they have been fairly and appropriately applied in any given situation.

Welfare in Canada: The Tangled Safety Net
National Council of Welfare, Ottawa,
November 1987

☐

. . .

Leslie is a small woman about fifty years of age. She has a disability that makes part of her body paralyzed. A doctor has offered her a possible cure and plastic surgery. Leslie told me that she has postponed the surgery, that she is scared to have it done.

I thought perhaps she was scared of the operation, but that wasn't the problem. She said she was scared that if the operation was a success, she would then be classed as employable, and her welfare cheque would be $50 a month less. At her age and with her limited skills, jobs are hard to find. She said that even with her present welfare of $439 she wasn't eating properly. If it was cut any more, she would have to go to the soup lines, and she didn't want to do that.

She is right. That's the policy—if she gets well, her cheque will be cut, and possibly her medical coverage. In the 1600s and 1700s, people deliberately maimed themselves or their children so they could beg and not starve. In B.C. today, the situation is depressingly similar.

. . .

Janice is in her mid-thirties. Although she has taken training courses and tried really hard, she has not been able to find work because of a learning disability. She has had some jobs, but they haven't lasted. She does many hours of volunteer work and is loved by everyone in the community.

Although Janice desperately needed dental care, she had been refused dental coverage by MSSH because she was classified as "employable." Employable people are not allowed free dental care—their teeth have to rot and fall out. It took a letter from her doctor explaining her disability to have her reclassified as "unemployable," so now she gets dental care and a little more money. The problem is, she doesn't want to be labelled "unemployable. She sees this like a rejection stamp that reads "damaged goods."

. . .

Pauline is a small, dark-haired woman about thirty years old. She was very sick when she came to see me. Her skin had a grey-yellow look, and her arm was in a sling. She was terribly thin, and her eyes showed suffering and anger. She told me that she had had many operations for bone cancer.

She was angry with MSSH. She needed a simple form to apply for a handicapped pension. She had been several times to the welfare office but her worker was never there, and the substitute worker wanted to make an appointment for Pauline on the same day that she was due to go into hospital for surgery. Pauline had asked for the form to take to her doctor, and had been refused. She said to me, "Fuck it. I give up. I don't care..."

I called the substitute worker, who agreed to leave the form at the reception desk for Pauline to pick up. Pauline's response was, "Why couldn't they do this for *me*? Why make *me* run around so much?"

. . .

Cynthia is in her early sixties. She's extremely well-dressed, with a coiffured hairdo, faultlessly manicured nails, and false eyelashes. Her voice rasped as she talked; she was recovering from pneumonia.

Cynthia had been an executive secretary for many years, and had also sold make-up. She was now on welfare for emotional reasons. Welfare had insisted that she look for work, and when she turned down a job she knew she couldn't do, she was cut off assistance. Welfare had also accused her of having "hidden assets" because she was so well-dressed—but the clothes she wore were from her "good days."

I contacted her worker, who said she hadn't known that Cynthia was sick, and that she had assumed her health was good because "she dresses so well." Cynthia got medical proof that she was sick and she was put back on welfare—as an unemployable person.

When I told Cynthia that the welfare workers didn't approve of her executive look, she broke down and cried. Her mascara ran down her face and she trembled as she said, "Is this what they want me to do? Do I have to break into pieces before they will help me?"

Should a woman have to dress in rags in order to get the help she desperately needs? GAIN is the right of everyone who qualifies for it.

. . .

I went with Anna to look for a place for her to live. She was depressed. All we could find for the $250 rent allowance from the Ministry was a hotel room. The hotel was one of the better ones. It had crooked walls, worn floors. Yes, they said, they had the occasional cockroach. A toilet and a shower on each floor, which was really inadequate for the number of people living there. The room had a bed with metal bars, a bureau with broken doors, a chair and a small table. A small window looked out on a back lane, where a mass of overcrowded wires dangled close to the stinking Smithrites, and a man was searching through garbage for anything that was of value to him.

Anna took the room; I don't think she will stay there very long.

. . .

Beatrice and her four children had just survived a house fire. When I talked to her, she was shaken up, naturally in shock from the fire, and was staying in a transition house. Beatrice's worker told her she had to move to some-

Average price of vacant apartments in October 1994

Metropolitan areas	Vacancy rates %	Bachelor -studio $	One bdrm $	Two bdrms $	Three bdrms $
Calgary	4.8	352	468	594	650
Chicoutimi-Jonquière	5.3	295	379	441	478
Edmonton	8.7	365	432	524	593
Halifax	7.3	446	512	616	753
Hamilton	2.5	391	500	604	764
Hull	5.8	389	470	540	616
Kitchener	2.5	396	502	594	733
London	3.6	411	515	637	788
Montréal	6.9	353	439	497	589
Oshawa	2.7	481	590	662	743
Ottawa	2.3	489	603	742	900
Québec	6.5	351	450	517	586
Regina	2.7	271	395	489	583
St. Catharines-Niagara	4.5	368	519	610	701
Saint John	8.1	326	384	450	478
St. John's	6.0	413	497	566	603
Saskatoon	1.7	278	373	453	508
Sudbury	3.3	415	522	623	684
Thunder Bay	2.6	360	543	676	811
Toronto	1.1	517	641	782	934
Trois Rivières	7.0	287	358	412	445
Vancouver	0.7	514	626	815	957
Victoria	1.8	461	569	712	800
Windsor	1.7	387	537	666	678
Winnipeg	5.4	330	445	562	660

SOURCE: Canada Mortgage and Housing Corporation

where outside the Vancouver area, although Beatrice is from Vancouver's East End, her kids were doing well in school there, her friends were in the East End, and she did not want to move out of the area.

It was unbelievably cruel to expect a family who had lost everything to move out of town, just because it wasn't "easy" to find accommodation for them. I called a press conference to put pressure on B.C. Housing, who were then embarrassed into giving her a house in a project.

Beatrice, one year later, is doing fine, and so are the kids. They are A students in school, and Beatrice is planning to go back to school herself. Money is a problem, of course.

. . .

Marge is a single mom with two school-age kids, one in kindergarten, one in Grade 1. She is determined to "make it," and is sure that she won't be on welfare all her life.

Marge lived in a dump that was highly priced and near a dangerous highway. She had no choice when she rented. Recently she had a chance to get a small house with a fenced yard, close to a school. She was thrilled. The place even had a garden where she could grow vegetables.

Marge happily went to see her worker, who told her that the Ministry was really cutting back on paying moving expenses. The policy now was that a recipient would have to be moving into a situation where the rent was substantially cheaper in order to have help with moving. Marge would be paying $15 a month more.

Marge was angry. "Why would they want me to be moving to a *worse* dump? This is the best thing that could happen to me and the kids. Don't they want us to better our lives? Why are they so stupid?"

Marge borrowed the money to move; she is really in the hole now. She is pleased with her new house and the kids just love it. She hasn't got a phone hooked up yet—she can't afford it.

I saw Marge the other day. She was pale, with black circles of anxiety around her eyes. She had the two little ones with her. She told me, "I had nothing to give them for a lunch, so I was embarrassed to send them to school. I'm going to the church for help. I'm having to pay back the cost of my move, and there's not much left over for food. Sometimes I wonder if my kids wouldn't be better off in a foster home; at least they would have enough to eat."

I gave her my phone number and asked her to call me. But she said, "You know, I don't want no trouble with the welfare. I'm not going to appeal. They might get mad at me and stop my cheque. Anyway, I haven't got a phone."

. . .

Welfare for single "employable" people was just cut by $6. [In September 1987, the Supreme Court of B.C. found the Ministry of Social Services and Housing policy of providing people under twenty-six with lower welfare benefits was discrimination under Canada's Charter of Rights and Freedoms. The government's response to the Court's decision was to even out the rates by *lowering* welfare benefits received by people over twenty-six by $6 a month, while people under twenty-six received a $19 in-increase.] I can't believe it has happened. With all the money that has been spent on poverty research, the government has decreased welfare. This six bucks will affect poor women very severely. It's the margarine on the bread, the toilet paper on the roll; it's fourteen loaves of day-old bread, a week's supply of aging vegetables. It's five pounds of non-lean hamburger, five packages of macaroni with artificial cheese, etc., etc.

Fiona said, "What am I going to do? How will I pay my Hydro? I already eat from the food bank. Maybe I'll have to move back into the hotel room. You know, that hotel room had so many cockroaches, and the drunks would bang on my door. I would wake up in the night and find cockroaches in my bed. I had to share the toilet. It was so dirty sometimes the seat would have puke or piss on it.

"Why is the welfare so mean to us? Why do they think we are bad and no good? I'm fifty. I used to work until six years ago when I had a nervous breakdown. Sometimes I work as a waitress, but I'm just not fast enough. What am I going to do? I wish I was dead. I'm no use to anyone. Maybe I should kill myself. That would sure please Bill Vander Zalm. He would say, one less poor person to feed. Maybe he would like us to be slaves in his castle so he could be a king and his old lady a queen.

"Maybe I should break my legs, then I would be unemployable, then I would get more money and they would treat me better.

"Maybe I will see you next week, or maybe I won't," Fiona said. "Maybe I'll get hit by a bus; at least I'll eat in the hospital."

I told Fiona to apply to be changed to the unemployable rate. She said she already had, and that they had turned her down. I told her groups were organizing to fight this cut. She didn't hear me. I don't blame her.

. . .

The first food bank in Canada was set up in Edmonton in 1981. By the end of 1984, there were 75 organizations designated as food banks throughout the country. By 1985, their number had swollen to 94. The monthly distribution of food bags by the Vancouver Food Bank grew from 226 bags in December 1982 to 11,251 bags in April 1985, an increase of over 4000% in 33 months.

Welfare in Canada   1987

☐

Food banks have become an established part of making ends meet for the vast majority of people using them. For welfare recipients in particular, who make up in total over 80% of users, the food banks have become an essential part of their daily survival. 30% of users had worked, prior to their present unemployment period, in stable, steady jobs until laid off in the recession. Food banks help over 70,000 in B.C. each month, but the needs of the hungry far exceed the assistance food banks can provide.

Food Bank Users: A Profile of the Hungry in B.C.   Social Planning and Research Council of B.C., Vancouver, June 1986

☐

. . .

A young woman burns herself with matches, just little burns on her clothes and hands. She lights the match for a minute, watches it as she places it on her jeans. It burns a little, I smell the material scorching, and then she blows the match out. She is terribly thin. She hasn't washed herself or her clothes (what there are of them) for a long time. But she survives and chooses not to go for help because she doesn't (can't?) read. Her experiences of mental institutions have been really frightening, so she chooses her freedom.

. . .

An older woman has no place to sleep. She insists she wants me to get some tobacco money for her, from "welfare," she says. She has no I.D. and no money. She tells me she had psychiatric care in Ontario. She wavers in and out of reality. I can't get her to apply for welfare, or even to get an I.D. Every time I make an appointment for her, she says, "Not today."

. . .

It was a cold, miserable mid-November morning at 6:00 a.m. I was taking the bus to the hospital, where I was booked for surgery. A tall woman in a thin coat joined me at the wet bus stop, and we started to talk to each other.

She was the mother of two girls; one was sixteen and the other would be nineteen in January. The eighteen-year-old had had a part-time job in the summer. Welfare had found out about it, and the young woman had been cut off her mother's cheque. She had lost the part-time job, and was now totally dependent on her mom. She would be graduating in June. The woman said, "I'll do anything to get my daughter through high school." So she was going downtown to deliver flyers at six in the morning in the rain (an under-the-table job, of course). I told her that her daughter was now eligible for welfare again, since she was not working, but the woman said, "It's going to be tough, especially with Christmas, but I just don't want to fight with *them*. I always lose. It's better this way." So her daughter will graduate in spite of welfare.

. . .

The rules of the welfare system are often so unfair that people do not in good conscience consider they are violating the law. For example, a British Columbia welfare recipient was charged with fraud for not declaring $2,674 in income she earned as a homemaker between 1978 and 1979. She was sentenced to 90 days in prison and two hours per week of community service. This woman did not disclose her outside income because she could not adequately support herself and her child on a $440 monthly cheque. The Statistics Canada poverty line at that time (1978) was pegged at $638 a month.

Welfare in Canada 1987

□

In this province welfare is regularly linked with "fraud" and "crackdowns" by the minister of the day. Yet despite a 1983-84 B.C. welfare caseload of 127,471 people, the government laid only 205 charges of welfare fraud.

Vancouver Sun January 28, 1988

□

In 1994-95 the equivalent figures are: 342,510 GAIN recipients, 140 cases charged. The number of cases which resulted in conviction were 194 (including some cases from previous years).

Figures from **Ministry of Social Services**

□

. . .

Before Christmas

It's cold and grey; rain is threatening. Parents, most of them women with little tots, have been lining up outside the Christmas Bureau to get money from the Christmas Empty Stocking Fund. Most of them have bent heads to hide their shame at standing outside on the street, being branded "poor, poor, poor." As buses go by, they turn their heads away. They don't want to be here, but there is no choice. Their backs ache from holding little ones. Their feet are sore and cold. One woman faints. No time to go to the washroom—you might lose your place in line. One of the women has a new baby just three weeks old. Her other child is two. One baby is in a snugglie and one in a stroller. She is tired and pale; she doesn't think she can last much longer. (The average wait was two hours.) People are four deep on the sidewalk.

The next day, I met a woman at the bus stop. She was thin, tired and cold. Poverty showed in her face and her body: the poverty that ages a woman and gives her that grim "I've gotta survive" look. She had a stuffed animal sticking out of a bag. She said, "I lined up today for free toys, but I didn't bring the right slip so they made me go home and get it. I had to come back again, but I got two toys for my kids, and some candy too. You know, I lined up yesterday for Safeway vouchers. Christmas sure wears you out. I'll be glad when it's over, but at least the kids will have something." She got on the bus, a poor woman blaming herself because she couldn't fill her childrens' Christmas stockings.

. . .

The women's centre Christmas dinner. Lots of good food, presents, and laughter. About 100 women mingle in a small space.

Margaret: "Look, I hate to bother you, I know it's a party, but I have to know . . ." She was pale and upset. We tried to find a few inches of space in the crowded room.

Margaret's eighteen-year-old son had just started a job in a grocery store. The family's welfare worker spotted him there. Margaret still had him listed as a dependent and was collecting welfare for him; her reasoning was that she was still supporting him, because he was trying to save some money. He wanted to take some courses that would help him with his plans to stay out of trouble and get out of poverty.

Margaret was scared that she would be charged with fraud, and that her son would have to quit his job. He wasn't going to school. She was already under pressure from the welfare office—her worker had told her that her volunteer work was interfering with her job search and that she would need to provide a detailed account of how she spent her day. Margaret has had several breakdowns and has been in hospital a few times. If they keep pressuring her, she will likely end up in a hospital under psychiatric care. (And won't that cost the taxpayers a bundle!)

. . .

A six-hour period at the women's centre, two days after Christmas:

. .

"I'm feeling suicidal," she says. "I don't want to feel this way. I'm scared." Tears. Another woman: "I blew my welfare cheque. I got drunk and fell off the wagon. I've never done it before. I was so depressed at Christmas; I wanted my kids."

. .

She sits quietly sobbing; her hyperactive four-year-old daughter screams and pulls at her arm. "I need a place to stay with my child. I need a break. I feel suicidal. I can't call my worker—I don't want to lose my child, but I can't take it anymore. I tried to find a place to stay. I need a foster home that would take me and my child. Perhaps I should give up my child. I'm burned-out, I have nothing left to give her. I'm no good. I never have been!"

. .

"My old man blew our welfare cheque. I want to leave him; he is so fucking irresponsible, but I want him to get some help too. I'm going to have to go to a transition house. I can't take the fights anymore. The baby is only two months old. I don't know what to do—I love him, but there's no money left for the rent."

. . .

Jamie phoned me on a Friday at about five o'clock. A reporter had given her my phone number.

She was crying. Her cat had got sick and needed a vet, so she had gone to the Society for the Prevention of Cruelty to Animals. Jamie explained to the receptionist that she couldn't afford to pay the bill, that she was on a handicapped pension and her children were going to school, and all she had left for the month was eighteen dollars.

Jamie told me, "I couldn't believe how the receptionist put me down, how cruel she was to me. Her attitude was that I was a lazy welfare bum. I'm not. I'm sick. I'm going into hospital next week for an operation. I have a good credit rating now, but she told me my bill would be put into a collection agency. I offered to pay $5.00 a week, but I'm already surviving only because of food banks."

The same thing had happened to me three years before when Fred, my white angora cat, got sick. I too went to the SCPA. I was broke, too, in tears because of loving my cat and being scared he would die. I was told that I would have to pay $35 for three minutes of the vet's time. The shame and the low self-esteem that I felt in being poor and having to explain this in a crowded waiting room still makes me shudder. In the end, I had to borrow the $35 to pay them.

I knew how Jamie's self-esteem and self-worth had been damaged by a society that was supposed to be humane. I advised her to write a letter to the newspaper, and to contact the president of the SPCA and ask about the reasons for receiving such inhumane treatment.

Later, Jamie called me back. She was very happy. She had talked to an executive in the SPCA, who told her that the subject of fees and poor people was on the agenda for their next meeting. He took the details and told her not to worry about her bill, which was over $100. It would be taken care of by the society.

. . .

Linda, another welfare advocate working in the Vancouver area, told me these two stories.

"A woman called me on a Friday morning. She had been at a friend's crying about the desperate situation she was in, and a neighbour visited and gave her my name.

"She was going into hospital the next day, and she had tried through every avenue to get a homemaker for her kids while she was away. She'd tried the Ministry of Social Services and Housing, the Ombudsman, everyone she could think of. I listened to her and called a few people I knew. One social worker said there was nothing I could do on a Friday! There was no time to appeal or to get an appointment with a lawyer, and so there was only me. A real case for Super Advocate! I talked with her worker, the District Supervisor and the Regional Manager—all people I knew from other cases and had been careful to keep cooperative with. At 4:00 p.m., one half-hour before the office closed, she got exactly what she wanted.

"Another case was a woman who got maintenance money from her husband in lump payments. The Ministry allows you to keep $100 a month, no more, so they were going to take this money off her cheque. If she had been getting this money every month in $100 amounts, they'd have let her keep it. I prepared her case really well. We got to the tribunal prepared. I talked to the lawyer from Legal Aid, used the GAIN Act and regulations, set up the tribunal well—and we won!"

O

Surviving on Welfare

So it's happened: your unemployment insurance has run out or your partner has just left or you have gotten sick, and you have to apply for welfare. You are aware of the stigma and the prejudices against people on welfare. You feel ashamed. You hope your neighbours won't find out. Your phone and Hydro bills are overdue; you owe everyone money.

You apprehensively call MSSH and make that dreaded appointment. You decide to wear your oldest clothes and take off the gold ring. You have started on the downhill run of losing your self-esteem and sense of self-worth. You might even have to have a couple of drinks just to get your self-esteem back.

So, stop right there...

First, find a group that does welfare advocacy and find out about your rights. Welfare won't always tell you what your rights are.

When you go to the welfare office, dress however you are comfortable. Be yourself. Hold your head up; look everyone straight in the eye. You are not there begging; you are there to get what you are entitled to. It is not a handout. The workers there are paid out of the same kitty that your cheque comes from. Some of them have been on welfare, too. And if they didn't have any clients like you, they could be out of a job and applying for welfare themselves.

The receptionist may or may not be nice. Who cares? Don't let him or her hassle you. If personal questions are asked of you in a crowded waiting room, ask to talk privately if you prefer. Go with a list of all the questions you want answers to. Make sure you bring everything they tell you to bring; otherwise, your cheque will be held up.

When you do get to see a worker, treat that person as an equal. Show courtesy and respect, and expect the same in return. You may get a worker who is rude or patronizing; it won't help to call this person a jerk out loud, but you can think it!

You're going to find it hard to live on the amount of money welfare gives you, so you will need to find ways to stretch that cheque. Thrift store shopping can be great. It's quite trendy, though, so you will be competing with the affluent. Grab the mohair sweater before the woman with the limousine gets it. Try to give the capitalists as little as you can out of your cheque. You don't need The Bay, Eaton's, and all those other highly advertised stores. If you're not too tired (you probably are!), bartering can work, too—for example, one woman I know got a futon in exchange for helping someone with term papers. Women frequently exchange babysitting services, and kitchen meetings where you swap your junk and strategize about how to beat the system can really help. In many cities, welfare recipients are entitled to free facility passes to local community centres—be sure to ask your worker if you and your family are eligible. Food banks, as necessary as they are to people on welfare, will really depress you. Take along a notebook and write down your ideas about how things should be changed as you shuffle along in the line-up. Talk to other people in the line and share information.

And remember—welfare *isn't* enough money to live on. So it's not your fault that no matter how hard you try or how well you budget, you find it impossible to make ends meet. But while money may be available again, the damage that being poor does to your self-esteem can be difficult to undo. So it's really important to find other women in the same boat, to get support and share survival tips—and organize. Come out of the closet and admit you are poor. Join an anti-poverty or other political group that is supportive of change in the social system. Write letters to newspapers and anyone else you can think of about unemployment and lousy welfare rates. Complain, yell, scream—but don't blame yourself.

○

7.

The System From Inside: A Social Worker's Perspective

Barbara MacKenna

It is not the intention of this book to trash social service workers or blame them for the mess social services are in. Go any cheque day to a welfare office and see workers uptight, nervous, tense, pale and scared as they deal with an angry, hungry client whose cheque has gone astray or been cut off. The caseloads that financial assistance workers and some social workers carry are often totally unmanageable. One social worker told me she often has to make decisions about people's lives even though she has never had the time to really get to know them. She has had to testify in court and make recommendations regarding people whose lives depend on her judgement, yet she hasn't had time to really understand the individual's problems.

Let's not use the social workers as an outlet for our frustration. The government and the present system are the real culprits. However, social workers are taught from a curriculum that often doesn't work out in the community. As long as people are poor, we will need many social workers. But if people had an income that was liveable and access to other resources, then we could cut back on social services. I have met many social workers who really care, and they are tired of trying to work in a service that is so full of holes it could sink. One of these workers gave me the following account of a typical day on the job.

S.B.

I arrived at the office a bit late today because I wanted to drop off a message to a woman who has no phone. I had hoped to see her last night, but Family Court went too late and I had a meeting afterwards at Children's Hospital regarding a sexual abuse investigation—the girl is only three and was terribly abused by her mother's boyfriend. So, when I arrived at the suite this morning, I found a note saying that the woman and her kids couldn't manage anymore on the little they get on welfare, and that she'd gone back to her husband. I couldn't believe it. But it only took a second or two to realize that, of course, what other option did she have? Two months ago, I was called by one of the transition house counsellors and went over to meet this woman. She had just gotten out of hospital. It was one of the worst beatings I'd seen—her kids were still in shock because they'd had to spend a few days in care, and had seen their mother brutalized. She didn't want to lay charges against him and there was nothing we could do but offer support and a safe place. And, since one of the transition houses lost its funding, beds are really scarce. Politicians seem to think transition houses cause battering! Or that only hookers or poor women get beaten. Or that only women who "deserve" it get beaten and killed.

I got to the office in time to watch one of the men waiting to see his financial worker start pounding on the desk and demanding to see her *now*. When Judy explained to the man that his worker was seeing someone else, he grabbed the telephone and hurled it across the waiting room, narrowly missing this old fellow who was dozing in the corner. We have tried to keep this guy out of the office by having him pick up his cheques elsewhere, but it doesn't seem to deter him. This kind of thing happens a lot. The level of anger is incredible, and for good cause. People are hungry and frantic. And we can barely offer subsistence living. Income assistance rates haven't gone up for years—they just went down! There is an increasing number of ex-psychiatric patients who can't quite manage on their own and so keep getting evicted—two days after they've paid full rent to one of the hotels—with no refund. If we issue another rent cheque, the same thing happens. But for a long time now, there hasn't been what they call a crisis grant. Or very little. Each financial worker has a caseload of more than three hundred people and is allowed $200 for crisis money. People used to be able to get money for a pair of shoes, or help with furniture, in the case of a family.

Last week a woman stormed into the waiting room swinging a baseball bat and screaming at the top of her lungs. She was pretty drunk but coherent. Her kids had been taken into care because of her drinking. The two-year-old had been found wandering down the middle of the road at 2:00 a.m. and the older ones, three and five, had left the hotel room and gone into the bar looking for their mom. The bartender couldn't find her, so called Emergency Services. No one heard from the mother until she came in with the bat. I often have dreams that someone is going to come into the office someday with a gun. It's happened elsewhere and it's only a matter of time here.

So for the alcoholic woman, what can I do? All the alcohol treatment centres are full. She is from a small reserve, does not want to return because of an abusive relationship and bad memories, and would be intimidated in any of the out-patient alcohol groups or in Alcoholics Anonymous. I went with her to the Indian Centre and hope she'll meet other women there. My caseload is so heavy I cannot do any long-term counselling. I can't get therapy for any of the children I've seen who have been neglected or sexually abused. I did manage to get some once. But just as the child was getting somewhere, I was told no further funding would be approved. Our Ministry says that our job is to do the sexual abuse investigations only, and that the Ministry of Health should provide the therapy. It doesn't work out that neatly, of course.

When I finally did make it down to my own office after the incident with the phone, one of the financial workers wanted me to see a distraught woman she had in her office.

The woman was about twenty-four and told me she thought she was about seven months pregnant. She hadn't seen a doctor and wanted me to arrange to have the baby adopted. She was willing to sign anything, she said. She told me she was a heavy Talwin and Ritalin user but that as soon as she found out she was pregnant, she'd cut back. She said she was still hooking. We talked about her situation for a long time. She realized that she couldn't care for a child at this point and she was not close to her family. And besides, she said, she'd been abused as a child and she wouldn't let a baby of hers near "that family."

The patterns down here are so predictable after a while. The women I see—Native, Chinese, white, Asian, any background—have usually been sexually abused as children, raped more than once as teens or adults, started hooking and/or become involved in battering relationships where more often than not, their children are abused . . . and on it goes. And on top of that, the women and their kids live in poverty. There are several non-governmental groups trying to address these problems. But most people don't believe in "the poor" except at Christmas when everyone begins to feel guilty or mushy about the poor little children! As a general rule, my sense is that people still believe that poverty is deserved, or that if the poor pulled up their socks they could "make it."

Maybe it isn't surprising that women are poor. Our lives are seen as relatively unimportant in the scheme of things. Most of us grow up with the myth that we'll be financially taken care of by a husband. No one bothers to mention that most marriages end in divorce; that battering and abuse have reached epidemic proportions; that if we survive the marriage, we'll probably outlive our husbands and end up poor anyway.

I read an interesting book recently called *Lives in Stress: Women and Depression*, edited by Deborah Belle (California: Sage Publications, 1985). I've passed it on to my social work colleagues at the office because I really think it should be required reading. Maybe I like it because Belle expresses what most of us who work down here already know—that one major reason for women's depression is their extreme poverty. She puts it quite succinctly when she says:

> life for many low-income women includes unpredictable income, unrelieved childcare responsibilities, poor housing, inadequate employment opportunities, dependence on social agencies for the necessities of life, and the experience of discrimination and violent crime...Many mothers have no time in the day for themselves and many are forced to deal continuously with emergencies in an attempt to maintain family stability.

Supposedly, social workers should work towards empowering our clients. (While I'm at it, let me rant about the word "client"—it implies that there is an equality in the relationship, when in fact most of the people I see have no choice about seeing me.) It is difficult to empower within the structure of the system which employs me, but I think it's possible. Most days, anyway!

I believe in the old cliché, "the personal is political." But what becomes clearer the longer I work is that we can't just seek individual solutions—social workers need to be aware of the structures in society that maintain the status quo. I think it's crucial that we identify social problems like poverty, and realize what the implications are for our women clients. I say "women" because the majority of the people I see are women, and most government social workers are women. Basically, we need to understand the "feminization of poverty" and recognize that the work we do *is* political and exists in a political framework. What we need to do first of all is to really examine our own prejudices and beliefs regarding women and their poverty.

Every day I come to work and am confronted with one dilemma after another—the ridiculously low income assistance rates, child protection matters where the problem is often poverty, kids who are sick because they live in inadequate rooms and eat inadequate food, and on and on. Ministry policy isn't there to address poverty, and I don't think that will change.

Everyone was stunned in 1983 when the child abuse teams, family support workers, childcare workers, programs, resources, etc. were arbitrarily cut by the government. Was it ideology or money? None of the services were reinstated despite the opposition of Solidarity [a coalition of labour, feminist, anti-poverty and community groups formed to oppose the "restraint" legislation enacted by the Social Credit government]. Maybe if there had been a general strike...

The fallout from 1983 is still being felt. We have a mandate under the Family and Child Services Act to protect children, but the mandate doesn't include prevention. There are only one or two programs for "at risk" families. So basically we can only provide services to children once they are in care. You can imagine the level of hostility created by this. We bear the brunt of public criticism for our work (or lack of work, since our image is that of pampered civil servants). And, on the other hand, there is the often justified wrath "clients" feel because of our intervention. What is happening for Ministry workers all over the province is staff cuts, little coverage for sick leave or holidays, continual erosion of resources, increasing caseloads, and fixed wages.

No wonder social workers are looking for work elsewhere, or leaving the profession altogether. I don't think people realize how committed most MSSH staff are to their clients. I know that flies in the face of popular opinion, but most of my colleagues are attempting to work within the public welfare system to bring about change. A lot of us work on other fronts as well—in women's groups, anti-poverty groups, community and housing groups, our unions, etc. The direction of the Ministry is vague right now, as it's going through another process of reorganization. Who knows where we'll be in another few months?

Barbara MacKenna (pseudonym) is a social worker.

O

8.

Linda

Linda is a white woman, a single parent in her mid-thirties. She works as a welfare advocate.

There's a few reasons why I'm poor. One is that I'm working as an advocate for poor people and organizing poor and working people in my area, and I haven't found a way for that work to pay! I'm deliberately choosing to spend my time doing that instead of taking some training and trying to get a regular paying job. I haven't found anything I like doing more than what I do right now, and it's what I do best.

The second reason I'm poor is because I married a man who had problems with alcohol, and I took my children Steven and Melanie and left when the relationship got violent. They were one and three then—we've been on welfare ever since (almost eight years). I never wanted to leave them with sitters or at a daycare so I could get training and look for work (or when I did I couldn't find childcare that was reliable and cheap). I tried getting off welfare a couple of times. Once I had a live-in lover help me out and it was hell. I was so tired after I got home from waitressing I would push the kids away. It really broke my heart. I love them and I didn't have the energy to work and make money and support us *and* give them the attention and loving I knew they needed. The other time I worked as a camp counsellor and took the kids with me. I was like a machine at high speed—that was the most frantic month I ever lived. It's pretty funny, too, because the camp was near the sea; we had food and lovely campfires, but I was responsible for fifteen teenagers and my two, and it was hell.

I guess you could also say I'm poor because I left school. My dad was in the Army in Ottawa and he asked for a posting to Calgary because he thought a move would help solve our family problems. So they (my two brothers, Mom and Dad) left my sister, who was fifteen, and me, seventeen, in Ottawa. I was in first year university—the first person with a chance at university in our family. It was too hard for Jackie and I, living on my student loan and a low-paying factory job, in one room in the city when we were both country kids. So I quit and moved to Calgary and found a job. I always wonder...if I could have stayed and finished university, I might not be poor now.

I would like to have welfare be a decent amount of money, so I could think of it like a wage for looking after the kids. I'd love to be paid for all the work I do around advocacy and organizing. I have this version of a system in Canada where no one's, absolutely *no one's* income falls below a certain amount. The cheque you would get would be like an income tax rebate—some few would pay more than now—and the old people, disabled, unemployed, working poor, single mothers and students would get this cheque in the mail. No social workers, no fraud inspectors, no financial aid workers or welfare offices unless you felt you needed help. Counselling, childcare, training for jobs, and homemakers would be available to anyone who needed them.

Eliminate the high amounts Canada spends on military defence, the tax gifts and loans not paid back by corporations, the tax breaks the rich get and the welfare system, and you'd find the money to accomplish this vision of mine. And if it sounds impossible—eliminating slavery in the U.S., getting votes for women, and even instituting welfare and unemployment insurance in Canada seemed impossible to most people. It's like eliminating war. Getting rid of poverty in Canada and the world just means working for that goal and keeping on working for it. And I think, what more interesting challenge in the whole of human experience is there than ending oppression and changing conditions so people can live happy and free? I'm proud I'm sharing this with Steven and Melanie every day.

Right now, I could compete to be a waitress; I'd be off welfare but still poor. I could try to get government money for our welfare rights group and fight to be the one who gets paid, and still be poor. I could make myself go back to school (and still be poor) and get a degree or whatever, have a horrendous loan to pay back and then compete for a job and still be poor!

If I ever did get money I don't think I'd live very much differently than I do now. I'd still work so that eventually poverty was eradicated.

Who knows what political changes might happen? When I look back at the changes—big and small, gained and lost and gained again—that I've been part of making, I'd never have believed I had the courage, perseverance and hopefulness to do this work. Every time some poor person feels like we have power, we can take charge and not submit and be ground down, that's another victory. If this happens to enough people enough times, I think we'll win and then l won't be poor.

O

Dana

Dana is a single mom with three children. She has a GAIN income and is thirty-one years old. She is a high school graduate, and has taken a mechanics course.

I am poor because I'm on welfare. My kids are being brought up poor. They can't do the things in sports that other kids do. I just haven't got the money.

If I work under the table cleaning other peoples' houses, welfare will find out and stop it out of my cheque. I would like to make some money to buy Christmas gifts for my kids, but what if welfare finds out—shit! I tried working but the kids started acting up and there just wasn't enough money to survive. I'm stuck. There is no way out—show me a way out of this mess.

More money would help. I need a job that pays at least $10 an hour. I would like more incentive programs, more real help. The social workers just don't understand. You really have to be stuck to know what it feels like.

O

Ellen

Ellen's children are grown and she lives on a student loan. She is in good health now, after being sick for several years. She has four years of university, and has worked as a translator/interpreter.

I am poor because of an unfair divorce. I have an inadequate student loan income, and too-high education and living costs. Being a full-time student does not allow me to work enough.

Student loans should be raised and tuition fees lowered. Make education free!

I won't always be poor. Eventually I will work in a career, although by the time I graduate I will owe $25,000. I'm almost scared to graduate. Perhaps I could stay a professional student.

O

Star

Star is a twenty-eight-year-old white woman. She is a single mother with one child. She works as a waitress and depends on her tips to supplement her minimum wage salary.

My stepfather was always mad at me. He would hit me with anything that was near. He hated me. As soon as he came in at suppertime, he would say, "Get into your pyjamas and go to bed," even though it was only six o'clock. My mother would say, "But she has homework, and it's only six o'clock." But she was scared of him.

I always had to go to bed. I couldn't even keep the light on to do my homework. He would never let me do my homework, then the teachers would be mad because I hadn't done it. That's why I quit school at fourteen, that's why I'm poor. No education, no good job. And a lot of hate inside me. I'm no dummy, either. I survived the street. I'm only twenty-eight and I feel like an old woman. I'll always have a hard time with money. The struggle makes you old. Free daycare would help me, but I don't want no social worker messing around with me and my kid.

O

Leah

Leah is a thirty-two-year-old white woman.

To me, being poor meant a great deal of rage and frustration, a constant gnawing at my psyche. It meant having no choices, suffering from a loss of control, and ultimately I felt like a victim of circumstances. I lived with a block on my shoulder which spelled "This is not fair" in neon lights.

My episode of poverty began when I was twenty-six and had my son. I knew I was not emotionally and financially prepared to have a baby, but I wanted this baby despite the tough time it might bring.

My son's father was a man of good intentions, but without commitment. He walked out on me one month after my son was born, and I had my first feel of poverty. I was literally stranded on an island with no car, no wood, no hot water, no bathroom, no tub or shower. I had a useless gas heater and running cold water, from a well, that had to be boiled on the stove to wash diapers and for drinking water and washing. I was in post-partum depression and economic depression. The man I had been living with had stopped by a social services office and asked a worker to come out and see me on the island, but he hadn't told me that. I awoke one morning late, to the sound of someone rapping at my door. My embarrassment at having a worker see the dishevelled cabin, diapers strewn everywhere to dry (you couldn't hang the wash outside because it was *always* raining) was a reality shock. I felt humiliated, trapped and enraged at the mess I was in. It was the beginning of the unrelenting powerlessness I would experience for seven years.

I returned home New Year's Eve to my cabin from dinner at a friend's house to see my child's father fully moved in with a $400 debt—a new wood stove—and no job. (He would live basically from my welfare cheque, supplementing our needs with various odd jobs on and off for five years, until our final split.) But at least the diapers dried in the cabin now, and the dampness was gone.

Prior to my pregnancy, I had always been independent financially, although not well-paid in jobs, as I had dropped out of high school with Grade 11. I decided that I would spend the first two years raising my son. I could not rationalize earning $3.65 an hour to work and to leave my son with a stranger to raise him. Besides, I wouldn't be able to pay a babysitter with that wage. So I enjoyed my motherhood and my son, and some of the anger at poverty dissipated with my decision, as I viewed it as a temporary trade-off. When my son was sixteen months old, I began upgrading at night school with the vague notion of heading towards an RN diploma one day.

We had all moved to Vancouver. I had left my man, and had gone to visit my mother in Ontario just before my son's first birthday. In six weeks my husband (I use the term loosely) had found work in construction and a one-bedroom apartment in Kitsilano. I agreed to come back now that he "understood" my need for security. One month later, we were evicted. He had not talked to the manager of the apartment building, had sublet it from a friend, and then was told that no children were allowed in the building. We sublet three other apartments before we found a landlord who would rent to us. This was a frustrating time, dealing with various welfare officers and the reams of red tape involved in moving our files around. Eventually, I began my upgrading again. I was fully aware that I was then the responsible one in the family, after a series of my husband's jobs falling through. He quit and was laid off incessantly.

I began having enormous hassles with my rehabilitation officer. After struggling through chemistry, math and biology, which were hell, and various other support courses, I was told that I would not be allowed to go to nursing school because the rehab worker felt that there would not be any work for nurses in B.C. What was needed were legal secretaries, and I had above-average English skills. I was told to go to Employment and Immigration and get funding for a year-long secretarial course, and to put my name on a fourteen-month waiting list. I pleaded that I didn't want to be a legal secretary. Why should I sit for a year or more at the taxpayers' expense when I could be halfway through my nursing course? I was flatly refused, and they threatened to cut off my cheques. I had to comply.

I became more and more depressed and hopeless. I made two more attempts to convince my rehab worker that I wanted to be a nurse. I asked to meet her supervisor to present my plan in person, and was three times refused. At that time, I didn't know my rights, so I became more and more angry and frustrated. One day, I talked to a good friend of mine and she convinced me to go to the NDP. I did, and was referred to the Unemployment Action Centre.

The caseworker that I lucked into was well-versed in welfare, and in the red, green, black and all the other various shades of tape to be waded through in the Ministry. We began to plan a course of action. He suggested I write a letter stating how my rehab worker had dealt with my plans since the beginning, and include it in my file. We then met with the supervisor of the office; my rehab worker was conveniently not present.

The ball began rolling and after three months of a lot of legwork and frequent meetings, I was told that I could not be funded for a two-year nursing program, but that my rent and shelter could be provided. I would have to find tuition, transportation, textbooks, uniforms and supplies on my own. I suppose many people would have given up at the prospect of a $4,000 dream, but I had already won. From this point on, I was determined to get through somehow. I had regained some sense of control in my life. My choice to be a nurse, not a secretary, was granted to me in July. I had to find the money for the first semester's tuition and get accepted by September.

Then, nothing short of a miracle occurred. A teacher of mine from a year previous phoned me out of the blue. He hadn't seen me for a while and wondered what I was doing with my education. He had convinced a wealthy friend of his to donate money to the bursary fund at the college, and thought I should get some of this money if I was in financial need and if I was planning on continuing my education. I was totally awed. The way was opening up. I found myself calling the loans officer at the college two days later. She told me, "You will never make it. This is a tough course, even for those who have finances secured already. Most people have cars to get to the various hospital placements for all shifts. How can you do this as a single parent on welfare?" She told me it would be "impossible."

I knew enough about the negative attitudes of people in positions of authority after having dealt with my rehab worker for three years, so rather than waste precious energy, I went right to the top of the college and asked to see the principal. I explained my trial through fire, my intent and my determination, and he looked across at me and said, "Yes, I believe you will be able to do it. I will enter your name for a bursary and you should be hearing from the department within a few weeks." The registration forms were filled out and I went home to wait, after thanking my teacher.

A few weeks later, I received a cheque for $500, paid my tuition of nearly $400 on the first day of school, and was elated. I bought one uniform and a pair of duty shoes with the remainder of the money. I used the library textbooks until I could afford to buy some second-hand, and I hitchhiked to school for the first month or so, since there had been a bus strike that summer and bus service had not yet resumed.

I felt positive, charged and blessed. The work for the next two years was excruciating. I would begin to study after feeding, playing with and bedding down my five-year-old. My husband and I had split six months prior to my entrance into nursing school. He took our son on the nights before I had clinical experience, so that I could get up at 5:00 a.m. and get to the hospitals via the buses for 7:00 a.m. clinical. I had very little social life in those two years, and more was demanded of me than I ever thought possible.

My mother developed lung cancer three months into my program, and she lived in Ontario. I wrote my first set of exams on the day of her operation—they took half of her lung—and a couple of days later I flew to Ontario with my son, my father paying for our tickets. (My parents had divorced when I was eleven years old and he had not helped my mother financially. My mother died in poverty, on welfare, and lived in depression and alcoholism for a number of years before that. She raised me by working shifts in a factory, and I remember her exhaustion, but I especially remember our love for one another.)

I spent my break with my mother at her bedside in the hospital. She had oxygen masks, drains from her lung, a huge incision and a great deal of pain. Once she was released from hospital, we talked a lot. She wanted me to complete the RN more than she wanted me and her grandchild to be near her. She wanted me to have the chance that she never had. I returned to Vancouver, torn and guilty but highly motivated to make it.

My mother's health and strength gradually returned. I didn't have money to phone often and neither did she, so I wrote when I could and thought about her a lot. I was full of anger at my poverty and the difficulties and unfairness of being apart from my mother at this time. I was her only child. But my anger was my motivating force. I had to make this pain worthwhile. So I studied hard, receiving A's and B's, and paying close attention to the faces of my patients, nursing them as if they were my own mother, hoping to project this level of awareness across the miles to the care providers involved with her.

Her tumour reappeared the following November, in my fourth semester of six. She was told that she was a terminal patient, although radiation would be given to prolong her life and drugs to control her pain. Probably the hardest thing she ever had to do was to phone and tell me this three weeks prior to me writing another set of exams. But the good news was that my father was going to send my son and I home again to see her.

I was frightened, and filled with dread. I went to school and to clinical like a zombie, and struggled to be in control and responsible for my patient care. My mother died a few days prior to my plane date. I flew to bury her. I had ten days to accept, mourn and dispose of belongings. I returned to Vancouver, and had to get it together to write my exams, which the college had postponed to the last possible day, and to try to provide a Christmas for my six-year-old.

Everyone at the funeral had told me how proud my mother was of me, and that the only thing she wanted was to know that I had become a nurse. Granting her last request was also my gift to her. As a mother, I wish for my child to be independent, creative and fully developing his potential, to be a conscious and responsible person with choices and wisdom enough to take responsibility for decisions. I can only assume that this is what she hoped for as my mother. But mostly, the struggle against poverty for me has meant the development of a new set of criteria, goal planning, a huge amount of courage, and—the hardest of all—to translate negative thought processes into positive thinking. I had to often shout "stop!" to myself when the old tape of doubt, blame, "this isn't fair" played round and round in my head.

I learned the self-control and discipline to translate anger, depression, blame and "I can'ts" into determination, conviction and work, through meditation and reading psychology, philosophy and spiritually uplifting works. I found strong female role models and talked to them to find out how they became effective and creative in their lives. Through the support of friends, through trusting my inner voice, I set my mental poverty aside.

I've been working now for nine months and still struggle with the aftermath of a poverty mentality. I gained forty pounds, at times eating my way out of rage and hard times. I still suffer from low self-esteem, and wonder if my skills and knowledge are equal to the demands of my work.

In society's gauge of wealth, I am still economically poor. I don't have a car or a tape player. I have a thirty-dollar Walkman which keeps me relatively sane, and I can send my child to camp this year. I'm paying on some furniture, and look forward to the day when I can get rid of my scraggly, spring-popping, leg-gouging couch, a constant reminder of being on welfare. But I intend to never think poor again. I have faith in my courage to overcome external circumstances, and to know that I am flexible enough to deal with them.

I believe that people in poverty struggle with issues like powerlessness, lack of control, poor self-esteem and lack of confidence. It is not enough for a government to send a monthly cheque (far below the amount required to pay rent, food, clothing, transportation, etc.). There should be counselling in motivation. There needs to be adequate training provided, jobs that will pay enough to take one off the welfare rolls, and training that will allow a person to continue to develop skills independently once making a liveable income.

If I lose my health or my job, I may experience economic poverty again. None of us can fortify ourselves against fate. But I will not ever consider myself a poor person as long as I am able to plan, adapt to and overcome my inner demons. I accept the knowledge that no one can give me my self-worth or my self-esteem, or provide me with security.

Now that I have accomplished one dream, I have many others: to nurse one day in India or South America, to counsel people on motivation, effective goal planning and decision-making, to get a degree while working full-time and studying part-time, to write, to lose weight, and to continue to develop positive thinking.

From past experience, I do not expect goals to conveniently fall into place, but I do expect to remain receptive to the opportunities that come my way, appreciative of the support I receive, and rich in my thinking.

O

In 1990, 59% of all families headed by women parenting alone were below the low income cut-offs. In part, this was because only about half of these women were employed, well below the proportion for other parents. And among those who worked, many had low-paying jobs . . . From 1976 to 1991, the number of women who had children under age 16 and were parenting alone increased 66% from 267,000 to 444,000.

"Female lone parents in the labour market"
by Mary Sue Devereaux and Colin Lindsay
in *Perspectives on Labour and Income*, Spring 1993

☐

Alimony payments generally represent a smaller share of the income of payers than of receivers. The majority of receivers are from single-parent families and these support payments represent 19% of their average income. In comparison, the majority of payers are [single] or from husband-wife families and alimony payments represent only 9% of their average income . . . The income of payers is much higher than that of recipients: roughly double overall.

"Alimony and Child Suport" by Diane Galareau
in *Perspectives on Labour and Income*, Summer 1992

☐

9.

Fighting Child Poverty

Patricia Chauncey

This speech was the opening address at the Child Poverty Forum held in Vancouver in April 1987.

I am very pleased to be involved in the Child Poverty Forum because I believe it will give us a good opportunity to look at poverty in a number of concrete ways. It will also give us a chance to work on changing the lives that many of our children are forced to live. I don't believe it is naive to think that answers to the problems of poverty are simple, even though the problems are wide-ranging and devastating.

I believe that:

Poverty is not the fault of poor children. If children had a chance to choose, I'll bet they wouldn't choose poverty.

All children should have equal chances in life.

Our society has the money to end child poverty.

My own family has experienced poverty for fourteen years in a number of ways and at a number of different levels. We have been on welfare and on unemployment insurance and have gone to work. Many of my friends are women in similar situations who are living on welfare or are working for a minimal wage and trying to raise young children through the most important years of their physical and psychological development. I have experienced, not just in an academic sense, the impact of poverty on me and my family. I have also experienced first-hand the views our society has about people who are poor.

When I talk about society, I include politicians, educators, medical professionals, social workers and lots of members of the general public who haven't analyzed carefully the misconceptions about poverty. A misconception is an idea that isn't true but is presented repeatedly as fact. People who are poor are often stung by the cold, hard burn caused by these misconceptions. We are often left feeling guilty when we are presented with these facts.

Let's take a look at some of the misconceptions:

Misconception number one: People aren't motivated or hard-working or they wouldn't be poor. If they just pulled up their socks they could tackle their situation and make it better.

Wrong. It takes a super effort to get through life when you are trying to figure out how to provide for your family's basic needs without enough money. Each choice you make about money becomes difficult because it means you are eliminating the opportunity to make another choice down the road. If you buy runners that fit your kid, you don't have enough for food. There is a good possibility that you spend every waking minute figuring out where to find the cheapest food; if you don't do this, you won't be able to make it even minimally.

Realizing that sometimes you'll make it and sometimes you won't is very depressing. Having people who can make the choice to go out to a restaurant when they're tired, or go on a holiday when they need a break, tell you that you just have to "change your attitude" really doesn't help. If working on your problem every waking hour isn't motivated, I don't know what is.

Misconception number two: People who are poor aren't good parents.

Raising kids is one of the most difficult and one of the most important jobs there is. You can be damned sure that job isn't going to look the same to someone who doesn't have the proper tools, like food, shelter, adequate clothing and an environment relatively free of stress, as it does to someone who has these tools.

I know a woman who thought she was abusive. She was living in a small apartment with two young children and was on U.I. One of her kids is a very, very active two-year-old. The woman yelled and hit all the time. But then she was accepted into a housing co-op, and for the first time in years she had a bedroom to herself and one for each child. Now she isn't yelling, and she isn't as tired, and she is being allowed to be loving and nurturing to her kids. She told me that this is the first time since she started parenting that she has had any physical room to remove herself from under the children's feet.

Misconception number three: People don't need more money, they just need more skills.

Look at all of the skills being offered to low-income families—parenting classes, life skills, cooking for those with low incomes, single parents' groups and now even a computerized employment service. These skills are valuable, but they cost a bundle to provide. Maybe the money would be better spent if those who needed it could get it directly. Setting up services to help poor people cope with having less doesn't make much sense if you could give them more. People who live below the poverty line need more money!

There are lots of misconceptions about people who collect welfare, like that they rip off a generous social assistance system, that they are leeches on the taxpayers, and that there isn't enough money in the system to support the needs of children in this society.

"Generous" would mean to me that there would be enough money to make sure that children had the basics. It would *not* mean that twenty-eight children in this school have to be fed by community workers because their parents are put into the position of not being able to feed them. Women who are looking after children are doing a demanding job that deserves adequate support. The welfare system was designed originally so that children would not go without! Families and children on welfare don't have their basic needs met, and the result is an avalanche of costs to the taxpayer later on, through medical, educational and legal expenses.

In B.C., big business is not paying its share of taxes. We have roads built to nowhere and huge extravaganzas like Expo 86, not to mention lots of expensive ads in the paper, in our mailboxes and on TV as p.r. for our governments. Apparently what we *don't* have is enough money to buy my next-door neighbour cheap runners for her three-year-old. Somehow, that doesn't quite balance.

Another common misconception: if you are working, your life is easier.

If you are working for a low wage and supporting kids, your life is often harder than it would be on welfare. When you're working, you don't have help with daycare expenses, transportation, or extra food and clothing costs.

Finding work is difficult if you have been poor for a while, because you just don't have the proper tools to present what is considered to be an appropriate potential employee package. Try dressing for success with no wardrobe.

A twenty-eight-year-old single mother in my housing co-op decided that she would put a real push on to find work and get off welfare. She felt that a job that paid $1,110 a month would be better for her and her kids than welfare. She applied for a number of jobs, and finally landed an interview. At that point she panicked, because her wardrobe consisted of worn sweat pants and a couple of T-shirts. She didn't have any shoes but runners. She nearly gave up, but five other women in the co-op managed to pull together pieces of their own wardrobes and over a couple of days managed to produce a dress-for-success package, haircut and all. After a superhuman effort, my friend managed to find a job and is now realizing that with childcare costs, transportation, and extra food and clothing costs, she is falling behind welfare rates.

When daycare represents nearly half of the money that remains after you have paid your rent and transportation costs, you can be sure it's not worth the extra dignity that you are allowed when you work. What is so admirable about not making your medicare payments, having no dental care for your kids, and having your family live at what is actually a more minimal level than welfare would provide? Women who are working for low wages know that they could provide for their kids more adequately on welfare.

Although we prefer to believe otherwise, hunger does exist in Canada. That is an uncomfortable fact to face in the midst of the affluence we see all around us. Children have basic needs that are not being met on welfare, or even when their parents are working. There are hungry kids (and not just a few) in at least fifteen schools in Vancouver. There are not supports in the school system to deal with hungry, tired, ill children who are lethargic, can't concentrate on their studies, and have all the resulting emotional problems of not being provided for. There's an old saying: "You can't fill a child's head when she or he has an empty belly." Right now, there are only a couple of schools that even have lunch programs. In lots of schools teachers are actually feeding children themselves.

We have a traditional image of a soft, playful kind of world for children. We get to see lovely images of childhood on TV and in movies. I guess one of the saddest things about poverty is that the stresses on family life take away these symbols of the provision of love and nurturing. Poor kids grow up a lot faster. It is very hard to watch your child dealing with more disappointments and responsibility than many adults ever have to face.

Children become conscious of the difference between themselves and others at a young age and there is a lot of frustration for children who have no relief from the daily struggle. Trying hard to do one's best v ith inadequate resources and therefore not experiencing success very often helps kids grow up with a sense of hopelessness and lack of choices. Older children know that post-secondary education may not be an option, and often give up in high school. Images of the traditional teenager wearing trendy clothing isolate kids who can't participate in fads and consumerism. And we know that families dealing with high stress have increased chances of facing marital breakdown, physical and mental illness, domestic violence, drug and alcohol abuse, and child abuse.

Today we are going to explore child poverty and provide some questions and answers about ending it. These answers are not going to be about patience and charity but will look instead at ways of providing for the basic needs of our kids.

I would like to end with a wish list. I hope:

1. That there will be a significant raise in the welfare rates to recognize the real cost of living.

2. That there will be a provision in the budget for affordable housing for people who really need it, through the development of more housing co-ops and rent-subsidized units.

3. That the minimum wage will be raised in B.C.

4. That the working poor will have the option to receive income subsidies, affordable daycare, medicare and dental care, and rent.

5. That there will be immediate recognition by the educational system and the government of the special concerns of poor children, and that steps will be taken to implement a program to deal with them.

6. That a hot lunch or breakfast program will be provided in all schools whose outside community has significant numbers of low-income people.

7. That the government will recognize that women taking care of children at home are performing an important job, and it should be funded to adequate levels.

8. And that we continue to work together to end child poverty.

Patricia Chauncey is the thirty-four-year-old mother of poor children. She was raised in a middle-class Irish-Canadian home by parents who grew up poor. She hopes that her children recognize the effort it takes to parent in poverty, and that they never have to do it themselves.

○

"An estimated 1,265,000 children under the age of 18 lived in low-income families in 1992," Statistics Canada said, noting that was 304,000 more than in 1989.

Vancouver Sun December 15, 1993

□

Poverty causes vulnerability which can lead to domestic violence, child abuse and family breakdown. Poverty carries additional risks for children . . . It is a major contributor to mental and physical health problems for children . . . poorer school performance, higher school drop-out rate and a range of other problems.

Susan Pigott chairperson of the Child Poverty Action Group, Toronto

□

If the head of a household is on income assistance, his or her child is sixty-seven times more likely to be in a "slow learner" class than the child of a professional family.

Poverty in B.C. Sandy Cameron for End Legislated Poverty, Vancouver, January 1986

□

The provincial government pays a foster parent who
cares for an older teen $361 a month; a welfare parent
with an older teen receives $53 for that child's care.

Vancouver Sun January 28, 1988

□

In 1995 the equivalent rates are $704 for the foster
parent with a 12 to 18-year-old child, and $103 per child
for the parent on welfare.

Figures from **Ministry of Social Services**

□

Children on welfare are 1.5 times more likely to have
chronic health problems than other children, according
to an Ontario study. The mortality rate for respiratory
illness among poor boys is twice the national rate, and
for poor girls it's six times as high.

"Children in Poverty: Special Report"
in the Vancouver *Sun*, May 7, 1994

□

In 1973 to 1976, native children aged 1 to 4 years old
had a death rate almost four times higher than
non-native children.

**Submission to the Ontario Social Assistance
Review Committee** 1987

□

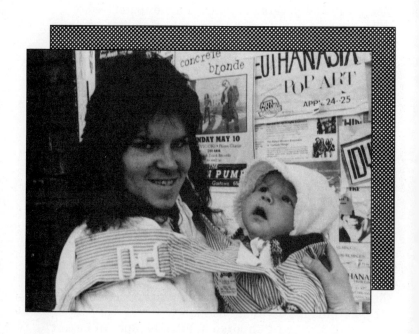

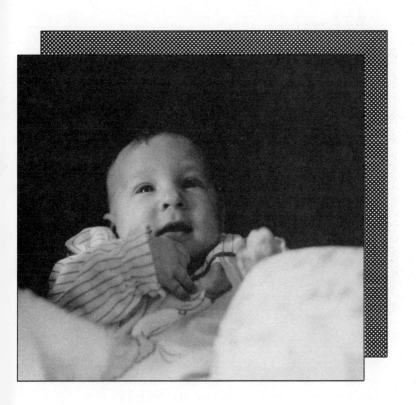

10.

Nicole

Nicole was born in Quebec. She is white, around forty years old, and the mother of four kids. She is a single parent.

I wasn't poor as a child; my daddy worked. I was his favourite because I had seizures all the time. When I was seventeen, I was raped. When Daddy and Mommy found out they made Gilles marry me. I hated him, but they thought that what they were doing was right because I was pregnant from the rape. In those days, a girl was blamed if she was raped.

Gilles was a bastard—see the scar he put on my leg? He beat me. He was always drunk. He threw the baby across the room. Daddy died, and me and the two kids lived with Mommy. She was in a wheelchair; she had had a stroke. We all lived on welfare. I took care of all of us.

When Mommy died I lived with a man from Haiti. We had two kids; we were always poor. Sometimes I worked. I like working much better than staying home. I worked teaching French conversation; I liked it. One time I kept my unemployment cheque at Christmas and didn't tell welfare, so I collected welfare and unemployment for that month. We had a hell of a good Christmas. I blew it all on the kids. Welfare found out. I had to pay it back; we lived on Kraft Dinner for weeks.

I don't give a shit. They can go to hell anyway. Even when I work, I'm still poor. The most I earn is $200 a week. I can't feed the kids on that. The change I would like is to see me in a job that paid enough money so I could support us. I hate being on welfare; I hate staying home. I need to move to a better place. There are so many losers living around me but being on welfare people think you're a loser anyway.

Will I always be poor? I hope not; it's hell. You know, it's not just the poor part, it's the racism that gets thrown at me because my kids are mixed Black and white.

○

Farendias

Farendias is a young Black woman in good health. She is a single parent. She couldn't decide which answers she wanted to give so she gave several.

Why are you poor?
I don't like this question because I feel that it assumes I'm already dead inside. Why would anyone wish me harm?
What do you think could be done about it?
I'll figure out who wants to hurt me, and fight like my life depends upon it.
Do you think you'll always be poor?
No, because I am resilient.

Why are you poor?
Welfare rates are too low.
What do you think could be done about it?
I'll participate in the fight for higher rates.
Do you think you'll always be poor?
Yes, although I'll be very busy.

Why are you poor?
Because the work I choose to do, raising my kids, is very worthwhile, even though this type of work is considered labour that is not worth paying a person to perform. Except when it's performed inside someone else's house, and/or with someone else's child.
What do you think could be done about it?
I am going to make what the society deems as desirable contributions, but sometimes I hope that others will

166

die miserable deaths, and suffer just as much as I have suffered in this society.

Do you think you'll always be poor?

Yes! Because I'm perfectly lousy at acting like a death-worshipping monster for any extended period of time...Wish me luck!

○

Kathryn

Kathryn is a thirty-four-year-old single parent.

Recently, I listened to a teacher read some excerpts from children's class journals at a public forum on hunger in Vancouver schools. These children wrote statements about their hunger and shame, and one child wrote of waiting for the next welfare cheque when the money ran out.

Listening brought back old feelings. I remember very clearly how it felt to be hungry as a child. The empty ache was so overwhelming that I had to fight to hold back the tears. We weren't always hungry, but I will never forget the times we were. I used to sit in my class unable to concentrate on anything but the knowledge that I would have to watch the other children eating at recess and lunch time. I remember that I isolated myself from the other children and watched them, imagining that someone would share their food with me.

When there was enough money for something extra, we had fruit. My mother always gave it to my brother and I. Now, years later, if my mother is offered fruit she refuses it. When she was young, she loved to eat fruit, but she spent so many years refusing it that she developed an aversion to it. I know that given similar circumstances I would do the same thing, nevertheless I feel guilty, because I think it would be better for her health if she would eat fruit.

I wasn't crying by myself in that forum. Other women, possibly women who didn't have enough money to last the month to feed their children, were exposing more of their frustration and anguish than I was.

I am uncomfortable with the term "child poverty" because it isolates children from their mothers. When children are hungry, it is because their mothers are hungry. If I had one piece of bread in the house it would be for my child, not for myself. This is true for all mothers.

(Reprinted from It's Time Women Speak Out, *House-wives in Training and Research, 2nd report, Vancouver, 1987)*

O

Sheila

Sheila is a white woman in her fifties. She raised three of her five children as a single mom.

London, England, 1940

"We don't want to sit with you, you dress funny and your shoes have big holes in them. And my mother says I can't play with you because your mother's always drunk."

Teacher: "Why are you wearing those large billy boots in the middle of summer? You know we are going on a class outing; everyone was supposed to look nice... What do you mean you have no shoes?"

The embarrassment of my poverty as a child turned itself inward: "There's something wrong with *me*."

Daydreams of being adopted by parents who would love me and buy me nice clothes and then I would return to these cruel school students and they would accept me. Of course, it didn't happen that way. I never did get adopted.

Canada, 1955

November in Quebec. It's cold—snow, blizzards and storm warnings. The new immigrants with their eighteen-month-old baby are scared. The job for the husband didn't work out. There is hardly any money left now. The child is sick. The doctor says, "Your child is losing his hair. It's probably nutrition—he needs fresh fruit and oranges." But there is no money. The mother is frightened. She is twenty-three years old, and quite sure that they are just going to starve to death. It doesn't occur to her to ask for help. She just assumes there is none. The husband finds a job at $40 a week. Spring comes...

Quebec, Before Medicare
The clinics, the endless line-ups in clinics. The woman in white who the mother has to plead with when the kids need medicine: "Yes, I know we owe a lot of money, but my daughter has to have these tests each month. She has been on medication for two years. If you don't give me the credit, she won't get her medicine."

By this time, the mother has four children. The family is low-income. The children are clean; she is clean too. She manages well. It's the hospital bills that are terrifying her. She starts to cry. The large woman in white says nastily, "Go outside! And when you have finished crying, come back in. Are you sure you don't have a car? I think you are just not trying hard enough to pay these bills."

The mother tries hard to stop the tears but they flow and flow. Her nose runs, the tears run down her face. The little girl who is sick says, "Don't cry, Mommy," but the tears won't stop.

Quebec, late 1960s
The mother is now a single parent with two adult children and three young ones left to support. Life is good; she has a job she likes, she is enjoying her freedom to grow. She isn't poor anymore. She has a car, a fridge full of food, a nice apartment, and life is a little easier.

Then..."Your daughter is very sick." She is only nine years old. The doctor says, "We don't really know why her kidneys are being destroyed." Endless hospital visits, endless hospital stays, endless medication. The mother is so grateful that there are no bills. Everything is being taken care of by medicare. She doesn't have to

plead with some bitch in a white coat to save her
daughter. She asks the doctor, "How long will my
daughter live?" "We don't know" is the answer.

Vancouver, 1981
"The house is on fire. Someone, quick, get the people
upstairs out! Is this the fire department? My house is on
fire! Oh God, please hurry. Everyone get out! Get out!
Get out! Oh God, where are those fire trucks?"

The fireman says, "It would seem that someone put
gasoline on the back of your house and set fire to it. It
could have been an arsonist."

The mother is living on unemployment insurance.
She pleads for some help from welfare. She is refused
because of the unemployment insurance. She has lost
everything, and has no fire insurance. All her savings
had gone into furnishing the house, and bringing herself and her family to relocate in Vancouver.

The mother stays at the YWCA in downtown
Vancouver with her two daughters. The fire has made
her a poor person again. The Y worker says, "You have
been here a week. We really can't afford for you to stay
here any longer. These rooms cost money and we
should be renting to someone who can pay."

The mother has no choice, no options, no power over
her life. She returns to Montreal with her fifteen-year-
old daughter and two shopping bags full of possessions. Friends mail her the money for the fare.

Back in Vancouver, 1983
The mother is attending community college, training
for a job as a financial aid worker. She graduates and is
full of hope, but doesn't get a job. The other older
women in the course don't get jobs, either.

December, 1986
The mother finally gets into social housing, after waiting a long time. In the meantime, she has been living in

a very cold attic suite which has taken three-quarters of her income. Her children are all married, and she wants to be independent.

She is so happy with her new suite. She is warm and comfortable, and there's a big park just outside the door. The rent is now about a quarter of her income. She knows she has safe housing at last. Then she reads in the paper the following quote from Claude Richmond, the Minister of Social Services and Housing: "If privatization is the most cost-effective way of managing social housing, then we will pursue that option." She makes a promise to herself that if they ever try to take her little apartment away she will fight them any way she can. She wonders why the rich are so greedy that they want even her little home.

The mother is now also a grandmother. She works as a volunteer in the community. Her income comes from a handicapped pension. She is poor. Why is she poor? She is poor because she hasn't enough money. If the system that she lives under had been supportive, if she had had options in her life when disaster struck, if the system of looking at poverty and dealing with it were different... The mother has given up the struggle and accepted her poverty, because within the present system there can be no other way.

O

11.

The Lighter Side of Poverty

Dorothy O'Connell

A longer version of this speech was given at the annual general meeting of the Ottawa Council for Low Income Support Services (OCLISS) in the fall of 1987.

I have been giving the lighter side of poverty some long hard thought, and I have not been getting very far. A recent article in the newspaper on poverty quoted George Orwell as saying that poverty was not only inconvenient, it was boring. The writer, who was a young single male living on welfare, heartily agreed. Boring. Nothing to do.

But the single mothers I know would not, I think, agree. I have never found poverty boring. It is, if anything, all too exciting. Is it today they cut off the Hydro? Will I get an eviction notice tomorrow? Will the landlord come over and sexually harass me? Will the co-op evict me for non-participation because I'm too tired? How can I get the kids to school on time when the cheap bus fares don't start till 8:30? Exciting, but not funny.

I asked my fellow workers at OCLISS about the lighter side of poverty. Their replies? "My purse is lighter." "My kids are lighter." "My cupboards are lighter."

Somebody usually asks me, when I speak of poverty, how come I always talk about women and poverty. There's a couple of reasons for that. Number one, I am one. Number two, so are my friends and co-workers. Number three, there's more of us.

There is a lot of talk this decade about the "feminization of poverty." Seems like these damned feminists are taking over everything. They won't even let the men have the poverty. But when have women and children not been poor? Think over the jokes, songs, plays of the last century. They are filled with references to widows and orphans being defrauded by banks, young women being sexually harassed and threatened with eviction by landlords, pregnant girls being deserted by charming young men, young mothers being driven out into the snow with their babies by indignant fathers. Go into any Irish pub today and a good 80% of the songs are still "love 'em and leave 'em pregnant" songs, and they still get a laugh. Funny stuff.

One of the myths we hear now is that we have brought our poverty on ourselves, by insisting on equality. If we had stayed good little wives, as so many groups are saying now, we would still be taken care of by men.

These are the words of Sojourner Truth: "The man over there says that women need to be helped into carriages and over ditches, and should always have the best place. Nobody ever helps me into carriages or over puddles or offers me the best place, and ain't I a woman? Look at my arm. I have ploughed, and planted, and gathered into barns, and no man ever headed me, and ain't I a woman? I can work as much as a man, and eat as much as a man (when I get the chance) and bear the lash as well, and ain't I a woman? I have borne thirteen children and seen most of 'em sold into slavery, with no one to hear my mother's weeping but Jesus, and ain't I a woman?"

Years ago I remember believing that the public thought of "the poor" as a fat man in a torn T-shirt drinking beer on their money, and if only they knew that "the poor" were really women and children things would change. Now they think of "the poor" as a woman on Family Benefits in a frowsy bathrobe watching soap operas and eating potato chips on their money. She goes out and blows her welfare cheque at night on bingo, and will have another baby in order to get a raise. Funny how other women go through hours or even days of agony in labour to have a baby, but not poor women. They just pop 'em out like that "Lay an Egg" game. It's cluck cluck plop, cluck cluck plop all the way to the bank.

People feel that it doesn't matter if Canadian women and children are poor, and that anyway their poverty is greatly exaggerated. A pundit from the Fraser Institute, a right-wing think tank in B.C. (where else?) was just quoted as saying that you couldn't believe the statistics about poverty. He said that some of those people are old, and some are young. They aren't poor, they are just at a time in their lives when they don't have any money. That's not poverty. And he said two-thirds of the statistics were these people.

There is a publicity campaign to increase the awareness of the general public about the issue of non-support. It consists of posters, bus ads, bumper stickers, buttons and novelty items on the subject of child support. As an example we have posters which say "Real men pay child support" and "Would you recognize your child if you met him on a bus?" and "Are you punishing your children because you're angry at their mother?"

One novelty item is a gift box labelled "OCLISS Support Hose." Inside is a length of black rubber hose with a bow on it and instructions: "1. Locate defaulting spouse. 2. Remove hose from box. 3. Wave under nose, uttering the following: 'Where is my child support?' 4. Repeat as necessary." There is also a footnote which says that in case of hose malfunction people can create their own by filling a sock with sand.

This has caused male hackles to rise to an alarming degree. We have been accused of promoting violence toward men. We do not perceive this to be violent. We perceive child poverty to be violence against children, condoned by the public, and affecting one child in five in Canada. Interestingly enough, the hose item does not use the word "male" or make any reference to gender. It simply says "defaulting spouse." But it is perceived to be anti-male.

Here's a poem from *Sister Goose*, my book of feminist nursery rhymes. This one is on child support:

Christmas is a-coming
And daddy now is due
All jolly, loudly humming
With a present just for you.
It's more than mom can buy you
As you've already found
Too bad it's only once a year
El Cheapo comes around.

Another way people try not to deal with the reality of poverty in this country is to take another tack on the "it's their own fault" excuse, and call it genetic.

If we had a smoke alarm that only worked four out of five times, we'd get rid of it. Are we really ready to say that 20% of the male sperm in the country is defective? But of course not. The quality of the baby is dependent on the mother, isn't it? That's why we have heard talk over the past decade of charging women with prenatal child abuse if they take drugs, or drink, or smoke. Nobody talked of charging the father. Nobody spoke of charging the government with prenatal child abuse if the woman had to work with machines that might be dangerous, or if she didn't have enough to eat because of government policy.

Because it *is* government policy to keep a certain portion of the population poor. The Conservative government in Ottawa made a conscious decision to fight inflation by having large numbers of people unemployed. Unemployed people are useful in several ways. Social control, for instance. Notice the postal strike. Government offered poor unemployed people the opportunity to earn $10 an hour with an additional $3.75 an hour—in other words, $14 an hour to be scabs and break the postal union.

Of course they don't put it quite that way. They don't say that the extra $3.75 is because you may get your face kicked in by an enraged postal worker who is facing possible unemployment himself or herself if the government carries this out.

But if we co-operate with that, if we help bust a union, we are selling ourselves down the river. It is through unions we can get some of the things most of us who work outside the home need: on-site twenty-four-hour child-care, maternity leave, dental benefits, compassionate leave—but besides that, if we let governments and big business have their way with unions, how can we be expected to get out of the situation we are in?

Martin Niemoller, after the Second World War, put it this way: "In Germany they came first for the communists, and I didn't speak up because I wasn't a communist. Then they came for the Jews and I didn't speak up because I wasn't a Jew. Then they came for the trade unionists, and I didn't speak up because I wasn't a trade unionist. Then they came for the Catholics, and I didn't speak up because I was a Protestant. Then they came for me, and by that time no one was left to speak up."

And we must lend our support to other women, and not try to bring them down to our level, but help them to attain a place from which they can help the rest of us. Too often, we put down successful women, saying things like, she's too bossy, she's too aggressive, she's too abrasive. And the successful women have to care for those of us who haven't made it yet. Too often, women are the worst enemies of women.

All through the history of women, while most of us were dying in poverty and misery, some were not. But few of those women did much to help others, seeing it as a matter of class, or caste. They saw it as God's will that there should be poor women to visit with baskets, while they should thrive, in their minds dividing the mass of women into "us" and "them."

Most of the lady bountiful feeling is certainly gone, but there still remains, among many fairly successful women, a feeling that poor women don't have to be poor, that if they weren't inherently lazy or stupid, they could be right up there with other women. But why do even some women argue that poverty is optional? Why do some women want to believe the myths about women on welfare?

Because the alternative, the truth, is too frightening. They realize that it could happen to them. Through no fault of their own, even though they've been good, they could find themselves at the bottom of the social scale.

Some women will shoplift before they'll go on welfare, will bounce cheques, will almost starve themselves and their children, before taking the last step. Because they believe the myth, that the women on welfare are the grasshoppers of this country, singing "the world owes me a living," and they know they've always been good little ants, full of the Protestant work ethic. The assumption is always there that the woman on welfare wants something for nothing.

Raising wheat is work. Driving a garbage truck is work. Raising children is nothing. So getting welfare is getting something for nothing.

What is welfare? How long have we had it? Have we always been "bleeding hearts" who support a welfare state? If we look at history, according to a professor of social work I was listening to on TV, we see that it really began after the First World War when, said the professor, society was shocked because those returning heroes had no work.

Well, right away I was skeptical. I didn't believe it was that simple. Returning heroes had been coming back for centuries to find out that society had been proceeding merrily along without them while they were away, and those who hadn't gone to war had not kept jobs open for those who had.

My suspicions are that this was the first time that the non-coms, the privates and the corporals and sergeants, were among the literate. It is easy to ignore the poor when they are silent.

The next leap occurred during the thirties, when young, healthy, educated men were out of work. Something obviously had to be done. Work camps were not the answer;

the men commandeered a train and marched to Ottawa to confront the government. Following the Second World War, there was another leap forward in social services. Each time, men were able to return to work eventually. But women and children continued to be poor, if they had no men.

Now, once again, men are out of work and getting angry, and people are saying something has to be done. But what will be done? Will anything really change or will we just get some programs which will temporarily fix things until men are working again?

And how will this be accomplished? After the Second World War one way for employers to give men work was to lay off the women who were hired to work during the war. When women were needed for the war effort, articles appeared in the papers and magazines about what good daycare was now available, glamorous women workers were featured, and recipes were quick and easy. After the war, articles on "latch-string" children appeared, along with romantic articles about housekeeping, child rearing, appliances, and recipes which took hours to make.

Coincidentally, articles have recently appeared saying that teenage girls aren't really interested in sports at school—their legs get cold. They are more interested in learning about make-up. And other articles appear about "quality time" spent with children. Guess which parent isn't spending enough?

Then, of course, there's the growth of R.E.A.L. Women. R.E.A.L. Women advocate a return to what are considered old-fashioned virtues. They want to see the return of the nuclear family; they blame sex education in the schools for homosexuality, AIDS and single parents.

But in one area, I agree with them, and that is the question of the value of work done in the home. The work that we do as mothers has no value attached to it by society. Well, that is not quite true. It is amazing how many people will tell you how much they admire Mila Mulroney for staying at home with her children. Nobody ever says that about women who stay home on welfare. Why should it be so praiseworthy to stay at home with a retinue of servants and a husband who makes a mint of money, and so blame-worthy to stay home and be the only responsible person twenty-four hours a day, seven days a week, fifty-two weeks a year, with no pension, no overtime, no benefits and no vacation?

For women on welfare, trying to change the situation can be disastrous. Do you know how fraud is reported for women on welfare? If someone is caught under the "spouse in the house" rule, there is one count for every month of receiving benefits while not living as a single per-son. The amount you are charged with defrauding has nothing to do with any amount you may reasonably have received from a friend, but the total amount of welfare you received during that time. So when the fraud is reported in the paper, the woman looks like a big-time con artist. I re-member a friend of mine innocently remarking about one case: "Eighteen counts of fraud in a year and a half! Why, that's almost one a month."

So picture Mrs. Hickman of Sudbury, who was accused of having a "man in the house" because of an eleven-year relationship she had with a truck driver who bebopped around the country and during that time had seven chil-dren by other women.

Mrs. Hickman had eight children. She got a year in jail, and the prosecutor appealed it, saying it was too light a sentence, and he wanted her to serve as an example to other welfare mothers looking for a free ride. The truck driver, of course, wasn't charged with anything.

How come Billy Joe MacLean, who fraudulently changed his expense claims, not only didn't spend time in jail, but is again a member of the legislature in Nova Scotia? How come Clarence Campbell, convicted of fraud in the Sky Shops affair, spent one day in jail, and a hockey team paid his fine, and an ex-Governor-General turned up at his trial and said what a fine fellow he was?

The Ottawa-Carlton regional government recently passed a motion to provide $50,000 to protect Ottawa social workers from their clients. Some of them will be behind shatterproof glass. But guess where the other clients will be? In the waiting room with their children while angry men who are frustrated by workers behind shatterproof glass pace around muttering to themselves and working themselves up into a rage.

Of course there is another new method to handle all this anger, too. One way is to assume that all the people who act out their anger are "ex-psychiatric"—the new buzz word—and they are sent off for counselling. If they're labelled ex-psychiatric it implies that there is no rational reason for their anger, so nothing has to be done.

As poor women, one of the things which keeps us from being effective is labelling. Some of the labels are so enticing we are taken in by them. One single parent told a friend of mine she didn't want a place in public housing because she didn't want to live with "those people." "Sweetie," my friend said, "you *are* those people."

When you're drowning, it's no good to whisper, "Excuse me, but I'm a little damp." You've got to forget manners and shout. What have good manners done for women? They teach us not to fight for our rights, to give other people the bigger share, not to ask what our salaries will be or argue about a raise because that's vulgar. They teach us to modestly pretend that we're not smarter than the next person, or better qualified for a job. We're supposed to cast our eyes modestly down, and let people find out through ESP how capable we are. We're supposed to wait and eat last, after everyone else is fed.

Well, we could probably stand the "tough luck, sucker" label if it wasn't for the fact that we go on patiently teaching our kids, especially our girls, not to push to the front of the trough. Do rich people teach their kids that it's not polite to take the biggest piece? Did Conrad Black's mother say, "Now, Conrad, leave some for the other kids"? Did Peter Pocklington's mother say, "No, Peter, you can't have another piece. Your sister didn't have any yet"?

This society says that nice people share, only bullies push to the front and take everything. And nobody likes bullies. But our society is based on a bully system. I remember talking to two young women who worked at Canada Mortgage and Housing Corporation who were upset at the idea of affirmative action programs. Is some woman after your job? No. Then why are you upset? Because there's no place to go but down.

Our system is pointed at the top, so there's only enough room for a few. In fact, I have decided that a graph of our system would resemble an egg. There's a small base of poor people, a large amount of middle-income people, and a small batch of rich people. Eggs are not stable. Do you know the secret of having an egg stand steady? You smash the bottom.

And of course those in the middle want the egg to stand steady or the shape changes and becomes a pyramid, and they're at the botton. But you can't admit this to yourself consciously so you have to pretend that the people on the bottom are there because they deserve it.

So what can we do? A lot of people subscribe to the Mr. Potato Head theory of government: no matter how you arrange the features at election time, you're still electing a potato. And such small potatoes.

But we cannot give in to this theory, alluring though it may be. We have to get our own candidates and elect people who will act for us, and if they don't act for us we must elect someone else. And some of those candidates have to be women.

And together, women *can* change things. As South African women say, "Now you have touched the women, now you have struck a rock, you have dislodged a boulder, you will be crushed."

Dorothy O'Connell is an Ottawa writer and long-time poverty rights activist. She is the author of three books: Chiclet Gomez *(Deneau & Greenberg, 1977),* Cockeyed Optimist *(Deneau, 1980) and* Sister Goose *(Steel Rail, 1987).*

○

12.

Shirley

Shirley is a white woman in her forties. She is an active advocate for the disabled.

Being poor and disabled means first of all that I can't buy equipment which is readily available on the market, equipment I need to live in this able-bodied world. At this very moment I am wearing a hearing aid that is taped together with masking tape. It was condemned two years ago, but a new one will cost between $400 and $600, which I don't have. Flashing lights that would wake me in the morning or warn me of the doorbell or the phone are also beyond my reach. I'm one of the working poor, so I have to get up on time in the morning. I have to depend on the sun to wake me up, but that becomes a problem on dark days and during winter months.

Captioned TV is another item on my wish list, but the price tag makes it a commodity of the well-off. I'd love to go to the theatre and to concerts where they reserve seats up front for the hearing impaired, but my budget couldn't withstand the assault of buying the tickets. Some theatres even have loops where you can plug in your hearing aid (but my hearing aid is broken anyway). So much for the pleasures of life! It's the real necessities that must come first, if at all.

It is very difficult for me to function on a seemingly normal level with my disability. Always trying to figure out what happened three topics ago in the conversation, coming up with great ideas that someone else already mentioned, filling in the blanks with the wrong

words and making inappropriate and off-topic responses.
I get tired struggling to hear and straining to see what I
cannot hear. My eyes burn and my brain aches. Just
trying to locate the speaker in a group before I can begin to speech-read is an exercise in frustration, since
only one of my ears receives any sound at all. Many
times conversation becomes so difficult I simply with-
draw. Often people get angry at me because I can't
hear. These same people would never get angry with a
person in a wheelchair who couldn't walk.

Of course, there are always exceptions. I work at the
B.C. Coalition of the Disabled where I get a lot of support. I am a member of the Disabled Women's Network
(DAWN) where I feel total acceptance and where I have
made many friends. But even here I must constantly
struggle with my disability.

My disability is difficult to deal with but not impossible. Most painful are the jokes, the comments that I'm
lucky I can't hear such and such, the impatience, embarrassment, anger and rudeness when I ask people to
repeat more than once. It hurts, it's isolating, it's angry-
making, it's bitter-making. Yes, I want to run away, to
hide, to find a safe place. The only thing that keeps me
even on the fringe of this unfriendly world is my hearing aid and this damned need to be with people even
when they mistreat me.

Hearing aids are not a panacea, as everyone who
wears one knows. They are exactly what they say they
are—aids. Many of us are helped by them. There is a
very long and difficult adjustment period (six months of
constant wearing for new users). The aid must be fitted
by qualified professionals after extensive testing. There
may be several trials before the right aid is found. At
best, a hearing aid can only amplify *all* sounds. They do
not hear for us. They squeal at us, they hum, buzz and
gurgle, and sometimes they fail us completely. It is
therefore important to get the very best aid possible. If
you are young, educated, beautiful, under forty-five

and can afford it, you will no doubt get the best. If you are poor, uneducated and over forty-five, you may be told that you don't need a good aid; a cheap one will be sufficient. Very often a cheap one ends up in the cupboard because it's no good. The cheap ones don't come with a lot of counselling on their use and care, either.

When I can no longer keep my hearing aid running with masking tape, I'll be completely cut off from this not-so-friendly world. I won't be able to work anymore. I'll be unemployed. If I lose my job I will lose my house, but my chances of getting a hearing aid might improve somewhat. After U.I. runs out, welfare might consider putting out the money for a hearing aid, if I can argue well enough that it might help me get a job and get off welfare. But then again, I'm a woman, I'm disabled and I'm over forty-five. Guess my chances aren't so good after all. Worried? Yeah, wouldn't you be?

One of the hearing world's favourite answers to my disability is to learn sign language. I am indeed happy that sign language has finally been recognized as a legitimate language of communication. However, it seems that well-intentioned people see only the beauty of the expression, while the complexity of the language escapes them completely. American Sign Language (ASL) is a very complex language with a structure entirely different from that of my native language. It takes years to become fluent in ASL. The twenty-five word vocabulary that most hearing people know does not a language of communication make. I live in the hearing world—my family, my friends, my work. My desire to learn ASL is not to leave my world but to be able to communicate with my deaf sisters. I must also ask, even if this were the answer to my problem, who would pay for me to immerse myself in the study of ASL to the same extent that a paraplegic or an amputee is supported to undertake a rehabilitation program? According to the system, I'm not really disabled—I just can't hear.

The bottom line is that I need good equipment just to live on the fringe of society, and I don't have the money for it. I'm really no different from any other disabled person. Our individual problems may be different but the issues are the same. We need secure and decent-paying jobs. We need health care services that are not petty and insensitive enough to put price tags on our lives. We need a health care system that would make available any piece of equipment or any treatment that would in any way help to ameliorate the effects of our disabilities.

I know many disabled people who are poor. Perhaps I speak for them when I say that I can cope far better with my disability than I can with being poor. Being poor gives me a double disability. Poverty drags me down. It defeats me. It takes away my hope. I have no dreams. I have no future. I hate being disabled, I hate it so much—but God, I hate being poor a whole lot more.

O

Josie

Josie is a twenty-seven-year-old white woman who lives on GAIN. Her health is poor. She has worked as a janitor and a cleaner.

I have no money; I have always been poor. My welfare worker acts like she knows everything. I don't have time to say how I feel. I would like to change my life. A lot of people are trying to help me. I quit school at Grade 7. I would like to be a nurse but I can't. But I won't always be poor.

O

Fanny

Fanny has a welfare income. She is twenty-eight years old, in poor health, and has a Grade 12 education.

I am poor because poverty is beyond my control. There is too much greed in our society and I have never wanted to be greedy. I don't believe people should bust their asses to make some pig rich. I have never wanted to possess material things; I don't have materialistic values.

I wouldn't be poor if I could steal from the wealthy and share it with myself and others. Mostly I will stay poor unless I decide to become a capitalist.

○

Antoinette

*Antoinette is a white woman who is twenty-four years of
age. She has a welfare income.*

I am poor because of my own stupidity and through
making mistakes in the past pattern of my life. Abuses
happen a lot in various ways without people realizing
that it affects others. We should be helped with earnings and integration of earnings—for example, free
public transport, free childcare programs for mothers or
single parents.

I won't always be poor. I have done it, I can do it
again and I *will* do it again. Hopefully I will learn valuable lessons about humanity.

○

Jean

Jean has worked many years in the struggle to raise welfare rates to poverty level. She is a single mom.

When you are on welfare, you are powerless. You are always at someone else's mercy and you feel very vulnerable, no matter who you are. Welfare is the last resort. If the last resort doesn't come through, then you go hungry, the landlord kicks you out and, worse, the kids suffer.

I was on welfare for about two months fifteen years ago. I went to the welfare office about four times. Each time I cried. I think I have repressed most of my feelings about it now, but I do remember being so resentful that they were forcing me to deal with my ex-husband, who I did not want to see at all, and I remember that I couldn't stand dealing with them. I went out and found another woman to exploit, taking care of my kids for free, basically, and I went to work washing toilet bowls in a motel. I think this is what welfare laws are supposed to do—to force people to work at *anything*, even though there is no benefit for the family and I think it's harder on the kids, because their mom is always tired and unable to give them the kind of attention they need extra amounts of if they are going to live in poverty.

I have to say this is not the fault of social workers, it's the system they have to administer. If they didn't, they'd be fired and then they'd be on welfare too. Systems are insidious for extracting behaviour that good people of their own free will would shun. I have been in a similar situation myself. I had a job slinging beer. When I knew that the patrons in the pub wanted five fresh beer, the owner would say to take ten, so I did. And the customers, being good working people, knew the tray was heavy and they'd take the beer off so I wouldn't have to pack so much, and they'd drink it. I knew the booze wasn't good for them. I knew they were becoming alcoholics. I knew I was contributing to it. But if I didn't take ten beer, I'd have been fired, and then I'd be on welfare again with my two kids. That's how a bad system makes you do things you don't want to do.

O

Anne

Anne has a welfare income. She is a white woman, thirty-eight years of age. She has a Grade 12 education and has worked in sales, reception and modelling.

I am poor because of lack of education. Education does not guarantee a job, but it helps. I have not got enough money to live on. I feel my motivation has been stifled; perhaps it was the loss of a parent figure—the breadwinner—when young.

What would make it different? If we could do away with money altogether and have free education. If we were taught that everyone is equal. If we could have real breaks for people, instead of getting them to work in rehab centres for $1 an hour.

If everyone were poor, I would feel okay. Everyone should be poor, then we would all be equal. I sure as hell hope I won't always be poor, but I don't know. Oh, poverty isn't fair!

O

Lorna

Lorna is a white woman in her mid-fifties.

After working for thirty-three years building up a business, going into bankruptcy because of bad health was one of the hardest things I had to cope with this past year. I felt useless with no self-worth. Then to have to go to welfare after all of this is almost too much for one person to deal with. I went into extreme depression, crying lots with no self-respect at all. After having a home and raising children to be self-reliant, it is very difficult to ask for handouts. I cannot even pay my rent on my welfare shelter payment of $250 a month, so my food money goes towards my rent, and food banks and women's centres become a way of life if a person is to eat at all. Definitely no room for any kind of luxuries. Thank God for support groups to help us get through all of this. I really feel there is no way a person can get by on what the government gives on welfare. There seems to be no consideration of how hard a person has worked in the past. You are made to feel like a beggar.

Changes I would like to see: doctors helping their patients and standing by them. Social workers making us feel more like they care, and welfare rates going up to help the poor cope a bit easier. Help to find affordable housing that is not rundown and full of bugs. More support groups to help people get on with their lives in a positive way. Help for people to get active in volunteer work around the city, encouraging others and themselves that life is okay, that we are okay.

O

195

13.

Single Moms and Social Change

Jean Swanson

The following speech was given in October 1987 at a YWCA single mother's symposium in Vancouver.

Single mothers have a lot to fight for, mostly for our kids and for more money. And sometimes, I've found, it makes life a bit better if we try to fight for changes in our society and economy that help all of our sisters and their kids, rather than simply trying to cope with our own lives alone.

The statistics say that 60% of single parent mothers under thirty-five live in poverty. The main problem I've faced as a single parent is lack of money. There are lots of other problems, mind you, but most of them stem from that one.

For example, I remember back to:

all the arguments that I wouldn't have had with my kids if I wasn't trying to get them to lug the laundry with me for eight blocks so we could save bus fare...

the good time we could have had going to the Aquarium together, but I stood outside and let them go in alone so we could have my fee for hot dogs...

the innocent little question, "Can I have money for milk, Mom?" and I'd say no and feel awful...

and clothes...I'd say, "What if I made you something nice?" and they'd say, "Mom, I don't want to look like a curtain!"...

shopping—I'd get so mad at food prices that the kids would refuse to be in the same aisle with me at Safeway...

our house—I later realized that the kids would have loved to live in a house that didn't have peeling paint...

and when I thought it was marvelous just to have a car, they wanted one without four dented fenders and one door wired shut. And they were embarrassed when we had to park it on a hill...

all the yelling at them to be quiet because my bedroom was in the living room and I wanted to go to bed early...

the cat having to go the vet when she was sick. This was one of the worst things—the kids would be freaking out that the cat would die and I would be thinking of the $80 or $200 that we wouldn't have for the rent.

All these things that increased the stress level in our household, and lots of others, I'm sure, could have been prevented with a little money.

Now, there are two ways of looking at this. One is that we single parents can take budgeting lessons and coping lessons so we'll be able to function better and get by on less than everyone else has. And that's okay, because we all have our immediate lives to deal with. Sometimes these things are very helpful.

But we deserve more. We deserve a decent standard of living. A society *without* poverty, not one where our best hope is to learn how to cope with poverty. And we're going to have to fight hard to get it.

I want to talk about how we single parents can look at our personal experiences, the ones we share with our sister single parents, and ask the right questions about these experiences—questions that will help us understand that we're not alone, we're not to blame, we're not stupid. Questions that will give us the answers we need so we can work to end poverty and so our kids will have a better life.

I want to share a few personal experiences that helped me move from personal hardship to political action for change.

If you have older kids, you've probably done this one.

Say it's the end of the month and you've got to watch your pennies. You figure out the dinner menu so the kids will get a little protein—maybe macaroni and cheese and milk—but, naturally, you're short on the cheese and milk.

So while the kids aren't around, you mix the powdered milk and sneak it into the real milk carton and put it on the table. The kids pour a glass of milk, take a gulp and go, "*Blech!* Mom, you mixed it again!" And you want them to drink it for the protein. And they don't want to drink it because it tastes awful. And you're out of chocolate to disguise it with. You say, "Well, drink it anyway." They refuse. A battle looms and you think, boy, do I need a course in creative parenting.

But actually, this personal problem is faced by 35,000 single parents in B.C. who are on welfare and living at half the poverty line. It's faced by tens of thousands who work at very low wages or who try to survive on unemployment insurance.

So what we really need is more money—higher welfare rates, higher minimum wages, wages for raising our children, equal pay for work of equal value. Then we could buy real milk and wouldn't have to take a course on how to cope with the problem. More importantly, our kids would get the protein they need, and face a society, when they grow up, where things are more equal and they have a better chance for a decent life.

So, maybe you get together with other women and ask the question, "How can I get my kids to drink powdered milk, or at least keep from fighting when they won't?" And you have a discussion and people have hints that have worked for them. That is helpful. I'm not knocking it. But it's not enough. It's also important to ask, "Why are welfare rates and wages so low?" and "Why aren't we getting equal pay?" and "How can we work together to start changing things?" The questions you ask change from the personal—"How do I change myself so I don't fight with my kids?"—to the political—"What can I do with others to make sure my kids have enough?"

And then you can get into action. You could join the Child Poverty Action Committee, for example, a group of women working to get food to hungry kids. If you did, you could monitor the School Board's hunger committee. Write briefs. Stand up in front of City Council and read the briefs. Talk to the media. Meet with politicians. Try to get changes.

Here's another example. When I was twenty-two I lived in the States. I got home from work one day and my baby was sick. By about 11:00 p.m., I had no luck in getting a doctor to come, and I realized my baby was very sick and so I took him to the local hospital. The hospital had a locked door with a little barred window in it. We pounded on the door and a nurse came and opened the window, and asked if we had insurance. We didn't—and she said "Sorry," and shut the door. We kept pounding and finally she did let us in but there was no doctor. And she didn't get one. To make a long story short, it was 2:00 or 3:00 a.m. before we had the sense to call my dad who came and raised hell and said he'd pay and got a doctor. But it was too late. The baby had meningitis, and he died.

For about five years afterward, I hated all the doctors who wouldn't come. And I really hated the nurse. At night in my nightmares, I'd see her face behind the little barred window and the window slamming shut. When I was awake, I would mentally compose hate letters to this woman. "If only you had let us in and called a doctor, my baby would be alive," the letter would say. I thought of it as this woman's personal fault that my baby was dead.

Years later we came to Canada and my daughter was born with a hole in her heart. We still had no decent insurance and we were still broke. I met another nurse at Vancouver General Hospital and she told me how to get B.C. Medical to pay for everything. And when I—being from the States—was dumbfounded that I would actually be able to afford insurance for a baby with a hole in her heart who was in hospital, the nurse said—I still remember her exact words—"That's all right, dear, our job is to help sick people."

Now, I did learn some personal things from these experiences. Like: when in doubt, demand a doctor. If you think a doctor won't see your kid, lie about the temperature. Be assertive like a pit bull. But in retrospect, I know that the individual behaviour of the two different nurses didn't account for the fact that one of my children was alive and the other dead. Now I realize that those two nurses had totally different job descriptions. The first worked in a profit-making hospital; that was the primary purpose of the hospital and she could have been risking her job just by letting us in. The second one worked in a hospital where, as she described it, her job was to help sick people.

So now I don't have nightmares about the nurse behind the barred window. But I do think about the millions and millions of Americans who can't afford medical care. And I know very concretely what that means for them and that some of them die because of it. Now when I have nightmares it's about Peter Dueck, the B.C. Minister of Health, saying that we need user fees here, and cutting back on beds at Children's Hospital.

If I thought of these incidents in a personal way, I would be seeking solutions like making sure that nurses have training programs so they will let patients into hospital when they're sick. Experiencing it as a problem shared by millions means that you look at the *system* and how to change that. So the question becomes, "What can we do to ensure that we keep and improve our universal medical care system?" That means action. It means raising a ruckus about user fees. It means fighting changes to the Drug Patent Act which will increase drug prices. It means joining the Health Coalition or the Women's Health Collective and working with others who are concerned about the same issue.

The mothers of the sick kids who can't get into Children's Hospital because of bed closures are doing this now. They're taking a frightening personal experience with their children's health and transforming it into political action—trying to force the government to put more money into Children's Hospital.

One area where I think it's really important to ask the political questions is in the area of work. A lot of people in this country of high unemployment rates are always asking themselves, "What's wrong with me that I can't get a decent job?" And I should say right here that if you're raising a child, you already *have* a decent job, and you should be paid decently for it. But if we want to get out into the paid work force, and many women do, we do, on a personal level, have to assess our skills, know how to write a good resumé and that stuff. But it also really helps to keep the unemployment figures in mind: 183,000 without jobs in B.C.; 75,000 so-called "employables" on welfare. There's a lot of competition out there and all these people need and deserve jobs. And if you or I get one, one of the others won't. So the political questions are: "What's wrong with our system that it tolerates such high unemployment?" "What really works to create jobs?" "Is the trickle-down theory, where you give more to corporations and hope they'll create jobs, working? Or do we need more direct job creation?" "How can I work with others to get jobs created?"

Maybe you'll want to get involved with a political party or an unemployment action centre or a group like Womenskills that works for jobs for women.

Changing personal experiences into political ones is also something you can get your kids involved in. Our cat, Marmalade, died, and the vet said it was from eating dry cat food which wrecked his kidneys. My child, of course, had fallen for the Purina TV ad which said: "So complete all you add is love." And my daughter loved her cat. So we fed it dry Purina cat food. Then the cat was dead and my daughter was crestfallen and moping around, and I said, "I wonder if there are laws about pet food having to be safe?" So she wrote a great letter to the Purina company suggesting that the label on their dry cat food contain a skull and crossbones and a warning:"This food may be hazardous to your pet's health." And she wrote to a couple of government departments. Now, we didn't actually change anything. But she got some letters back, and learned a lesson about advertising.

Joan Meister, a Vancouver woman, couldn't get into CRAB park in her wheelchair. That was a personal problem. But she didn't deal with it by trying to scrape together enough money for a cab every time she wants to go there—she filed a human rights complaint. And when the Port Authority retaliated by investigating her personal life, they took on the wrong person. She got together some allies, demanded and received an apology from the Port, and laid harassment charges against the Port's police. I doubt if anyone in a government agency will voluntarily tangle with her again, and maybe, if she wins, the Port will have to put in a decent access route to the park and all the disabled will be able to get there.

Ironically, when I look back on these years of being a single parent, seeing personal experiences from a political viewpoint has ended up helping me in personal ways.

Before I started learning about changing our society, I pretty much felt that I was always at the mercy of something: job schedules, or lack of money, or my ex-husband, or exhaustion. But thinking politically helps you become a doer. You start changing things yourself, and don't spend so much energy adapting to situations that others create.

Transforming personal experiences to political ones has other personal advantages. It takes your mind off yourself; you stop feeling sorry for yourself. You realize you have thousands of allies—the 35,000 other single parents on welfare, the 183,000 on unemployment insurance, the mothers of sick children. It's also fascinating. It takes you out of the house; gets you learning things and meeting other people. Lastly, working with others, you might just help make some of the changes that will be needed to give your kids a better chance—and this will make you feel good about yourself. If you are interested in taking this approach, here are a few tips that might help.

You *are* up to it. Women are strong. You've been

through childbirth, taken care of your kids while you were sick, worked all day dealing with your kids after being up all night with one of them. You're smart—you know where to get cheap food, and where the good rummage sales are. You can probably do several things at once, like bake bread, do the laundry, keep kids happy. Anyone who can do all this can stand up to a politician—you can even become one.

Secondly, you can't get any fundamental changes working alone. That means you work with others, which means meetings. We should be demanding bus fare and childcare or money for childcare when we need it to participate as citizens getting the changes we need. You can be nice in demanding this—the first time at least. Find some allies. Make a motion: "I move that bus fare and childcare be provided to women who need it." This is perfectly legitimate and, in my experience, if you're in a half-decent group, you'll win.

Third, you need to have realistic expectations of what you can accomplish. Sometimes this is hard. You pour your heart out in a letter to Claude Richmond [Minister of Social Services and Housing] and get a letter back from his information secretary saying that your letter will be brought to his attention in the future. You organize a meeting and nobody comes. You go to Victoria to lobby MLAs and even though reason, logic and passion are flowing forth from your mouth, they don't hear what you're saying. But each time you learn something, and next time you'll be better. Sometimes your work takes years to have an impact. Sometimes—the case of the Child Poverty Action Committee is a good example—you raise an issue and others try to take it away from you and dilute it or refer it to a committee, and you have to hang in.

And lastly, don't be afraid that you'll be cut off welfare for sticking up for your rights. In my experience, the reverse is true. When you become known as a fighter, no one wants to tangle with you. There was the woman in Nova Scotia who wrote a letter to the editor complaining about policies in the province's welfare department. The Minister retaliated by revealing confidential information about her. But she hung in, and challenged him on that. She took the Minister to court, and he was fined $100. And now she's getting her welfare.

Think of nearly any problem we single mothers face and follow it back with the political questions. You just got a rent increase. Why? We don't have rent control. Why? The Social Credit government abolished it in 1983. Why? ... Or you don't have enough money for milk. Why? Welfare rates are too low. Why? The Social Credit government hasn't raised rates by a decent amount since 1982. Why? ... Or you're working but your wages are low. Why? We don't have equal pay, or the minimum wage is far below the poverty line. Why? The government hasn't raised the minimum wage or brought in equal pay. Why? ... Your sick child can't get into Children's Hospital. Why? The government won't provide enough money for beds. Why?

I think if you keep asking these questions and keep investigating, you'll discover that the answer to the last "why?" of each issue is the same. The people who are in power in our country have a theory that private corporations will be the saviours of our economy. But private corporations don't like rent control. They do like low welfare rates and low minimum wages, because that means that people are willing to work for below-poverty wages. They say equal pay interferes with the market system. They don't like large government expenditures for things like hospitals, because that uses their tax money. They like free trade, even when it threatens women's jobs and Canadian social programs. In fact, just about everything that corporations like and want makes us poorer.

Women have made a lot of gains in the last twenty years or so. We have, believe it or not, better daycare, though we have a long way to go. We have more access to non-traditional jobs. A few men are trying to become more responsible, less chauvinistic. We have more groups, and we support each other more. We have more transition houses, though we need more. We've got politicians at least talking about peace. Women in unions are working for childcare, parental leave and equal pay, and these are important accomplishments.

But the market-oriented economic policy we face today is the reverse of what's needed to help women escape poverty, and it's coming on strong. And the experiences we have as single parents will wear us down.

But when we share these experiences with our sisters, when we ask the political questions about them, when we start working to improve conditions for everyone who shares our problems, then our hardship can become our commitment. We can be strong in fighting the forces that make us poor and fierce in fighting for our kids.

Jean Swanson has been a single parent for sixteen years, and is currently the co-ordinator of End Legislated Poverty, a coalition of B.C. anti-poverty groups.

O

14.

Lise

Lise is twenty-seven. She was born in Ontario. She left university shortly after this interview.

Why am I poor? I'm caught in a capitalist society that still holds onto the view that everyone is responsible for their own well-being. I'm struggling to keep myself above water. Due to the lack of job opportunities in the city planning field, I decided to upgrade my qualifications by re-entering university. Yet summer full-time employment has not been sufficient to provide for meals, clothing, or transportation, never mind entertainment. Lack of funding from the government has put great restraints on my life. I am not able to live above a bare subsistence level. I do not feel like a worthwhile person, especially when living among fellow students who do not have to take a second thought about where their next meal comes from.

The university's preoccupation with profiteering has raised tuition and residence fees, thus prohibiting men and women from entering or returning to university in order to upgrade their skills to get out of unemployment.

To alleviate my immediate situation, I have applied for bursaries and student loans and searched for part-time employment, but I am at the mercy of someone else's decision. Beyond my personal capabilities, there is a wider community involvement that can affect not only myself but others. Government priorities need to be reoriented away from big business to the individual. Why should someone be discouraged from attending

university just because they do not have the funds to
carry on beyond paying for tuition and residence?
Funding assistance should be carefully monitored so
that the people who are in need receive the funds, not
those who can milk the system for funds to support
their Christmas tours to Hawaii or Europe.

My greatest fear is poverty. Being a woman in Canadian society puts me at great risk—single women, single-
parent women, divorced and elderly women genuinely
live at levels lower than their male counterparts. All
employment statistics indicate that in 1986 women can
still look forward to earning a wage 60% of what a man
will make in the same position. Attending university
has been my source of advancement out of a poor situation—a situation I grew up in. I do not want to be
preoccupied with budgeting my funds for the rest of
this year or any year of my life.

Will I always be poor? Through sheer determination I
will prevent poverty in my own experience as well as
fight for all women to gain the rights we are entitled to,
the same lifestyle any man can look forward to.

O

Frieda

Frieda is a forty-five-year-old white woman. She was born in Montréal and has a nursing degree. She has worked in nursing, but at the moment her health is very poor.

I am poor because of stupidity, naiveté, not enough money, age, getting sidetracked, the job market . . . the whole syndrome. Once you are on welfare, it is less than the minimum wage and there is just not enough money. When you live below the poverty line you become defeated. I feel void and empty.

Job retraining and a couple of thousand bucks start-up grant would take me out of poverty. I would like to have a break from welfare. I would like some new clothing and decent housing.

I won't always be poor because I'll stand it for so long and then do something.

O

Ursula

Ursula is thirty. She is in good health, and has a Grade 8 education. She has worked as a waitress, a factory worker, a farmworker and a maid.

I was never encouraged, in work or in education, by the people around me. Even in school. My husband, the social workers—they all treated me like a dummy. There was never enough money to make ends meet. There are too many restrictions from social workers. When will they leave me alone, give me back my freedom, back me up and support me? I feel like a slave.

Free education would teach me to be somebody, and then I could do it on my own. I won't always be poor. Someday I will have money. I am going to be somebody.

○

Audrey

Audrey is a Black woman who was born in New York City. She has a Master's degree, and is living on a very low income.

I am poor because I come from a poor family, and I have no skills. This is changing: I am going to school. More funding and grants are needed while going to school. I live in co-op housing and I'm working, but I'm still very poor.

I don't think I will always be poor, but I will never make enough money to be considered rich. We need a real guaranteed income, higher minimum wage, more funding for education, more co-ops, more work skill training, and more access to information. Otherwise, how do you get out of poverty?

○

Yvonne

Yvonne is a thirty-eight-year-old white woman. She has a welfare income and is in poor health.

My emotional disposition and my present state of mind, due to repeated and prolonged mental and physical abuse, is the reason I am poor. I am currently seeking help from a psychiatrist and a therapist at a community health centre. I need retraining money, monetary support, a bus pass and proper clothing.

To alleviate poverty in general, we need:

1. Strong emotional support for the emotionally disadvantaged from community and social workers. Ongoing treatment for emotional problems. Further support to aid in re-adjustment to a new position in society.

2. Proper living conditions. Environment affects your mental attitude and contributes to a proper attitude.

3. Transportation money, and guidance for proper clothing and health habits.

4. Retraining or aid in securing a satisfactory position.

5. Financial and intellectual fulfillment.

Will I always be poor? That remains to be seen.

O

Diana

Diana is a white woman in her late twenties.

I take home $900 a month, which is below poverty-level wages for a single person. I am marginally better off now than when I was on welfare, partially because I'm subsidized by the person I live with. I would be quite strapped if I didn't share with someone who subsidized my income. Instead of living in an apartment which I can do now, I would live in a housekeeping room, and simply exist.

So, having a job doesn't mean you are out of poverty. I make too much money now to get subsidized medical or subsidized dental, so I have no medical coverage. I use free clinics. Making $900 a month means that you don't save anything, you know, and when you get unemployment insurance from a job like that, it's not much more than welfare. You have no security making that amount of money. When you take home $900 a month for a year you make around $10,000 and you pay $1,000 in income tax. So, I pay one-tenth of what I earn in taxes. It's like tithing.

I was on welfare for the majority of my life. I was on welfare as a child; that was really a terrible experience. It left me with an awful feeling about welfare, about being on welfare again when I was an adult.

I think a lot of other women have been in the situation that my mother was. My father died and left her relatively unprovided for, had $5,000 in life insurance because we were a working poor family. So, of course, this life insurance money was gone in a few months.

Almost half of it went to pay funeral costs and then that was it. Within six months after my father died, we were on welfare. It was a really big shock for my mom, and the depression resulting from her spouse dying meant she wasn't able to function as well as she might have been able to. She couldn't cope with the stress of not having money.

Living on welfare as a child was horrendous. Being in a large family where you know there is not going to be enough to last the month, you are not allowed to be children. You're aware of all kinds of things you shouldn't be aware of when you are nine or ten years old. You're aware that the rent isn't being paid. You're aware that your mother can't afford to buy oil for the oil stove so you're cooking in an electric frying pan.

We lived in a house that had no central heating. We were chopping wood for our furnace in 1968 because we couldn't afford to pay for the oil costs. Our diet wasn't adequate. We lived on baking powder biscuits and macaroni for the last week of each month. I'm sure that my little brother, who was three months old when my dad died, never drank real milk from the time my dad died until my mom died and he went into care. That's no good for a kid. I mean, he was brought up on powdered milk. You always had a feeling of being different. When you went shopping for clothes, you went to a church depot and it was during school days so you would be taken out of school.

You are simply robbed of your childhood. There were five of us kids. In the last week before cheque day, we knew that there wasn't going to be anything in the house to send kids to school with for their lunch. I, with my brothers, would steal food from a local supermarket. Load up the shopping cart and then go ask for lettuce to feed our rabbit, which we had. Then we would put the boxes full of lettuce on top of the cart and wheel it out of the Super Valu. Cartons of cigarettes and food would show up at our house and my mother would just have to not acknowledge it at all. Which must have made her feel awful, in retrospect, you know, to know that her children were thieving.

Our family was effectively split up by the social welfare system. After my mother died they couldn't find a place to keep us all together, and after a while they didn't make a pretense of trying. So we were simply split up and went our separate ways. I have four brothers. Now two of them are relatively dysfunctional—one's a batterer, one's an alcoholic—and two I don't see.

I don't think I will ever quite recover from it. I see women in similar situations all the time, and it's made me realize that I don't ever want to have kids, because I don't ever foresee myself being in a position to provide for them.

Now I work in a milieu where people talk about poverty; people talk about what it's like, and basically where I work everybody is poor, and the people I know are poor, and there is a commonality and there's a solidarity around it. When I grew up poor, I grew up isolated. No one talked about their poverty. There was such a stigma attached to it. I think for women, that they need to be able to organize with each other. The majority of my mother's friends were friends she had made while she was part of a couple with my father. My mother would never admit to these people that she was in dire financial straits. She just wouldn't. There was all kinds of pride. I mean, what stood in her way was the fact that she felt responsible for not having money.

I'm a feminist, and my mother wasn't a feminist. I don't think she ever thought in terms of being someone on her own. She was my father's wife or the children's mother, and it was almost as if when she didn't have the identity of being attached to my father, she sort of wasted away, because she loved him very much. Then she was also in the trap of being a mother of five children on welfare and trying to find a mate. You know, what man wants to take on a woman and five hungry kids?

Being a feminist takes away the blame. I'm a sexual abuse survivor, I'm a recovering alcoholic, I'm a recovering drug addict. I survived in the ways that I could, being brought up within the system and having been really severely abused. Until I got introduced to feminism, I had no analysis; I couldn't figure out why things had happened to me. I just knew that I was victimized. I knew that there was no way to get out of it. At the time, that's what I thought. I was lucky, though, in how I acted out my victimization. I put my hands through windows and I punched people in the face and I made noise and got attention and luckily I got help, because I didn't know how to ask for it. That was the other thing. I had never been able to ask for anything, because I had always been ashamed of either not knowing things or not having things. The last thing I would do was to ask anybody for anything.

But I started to meet other women and I started to think, basically. You know, I really started to think. I had to stop drinking; my survival depended on me quitting drinking and doing drugs because I was very close to dying. When I wasn't close to dying physically from doing drugs, I was always very close to killing myself, and I had been since I was a child. I needed to sober up first. I'm never quite sure how I did it. I was simply desperate and happened to have some people pay attention to me at the time who understood what it's like to be an alcoholic.

I think, like many people who've been abused and many people who've been victimized, I decided to help myself by becoming a helper. So I decided that I wanted to become a social worker, which makes me laugh now. I started going to school. I applied for a student loan and I started going to community college with the aim of going into a welfare aid program and eventually becoming a social worker. I couldn't keep it up at the time because I couldn't stay sober. While I was there, though, I took women's studies and I met some neat women and I got introduced to the concept of feminism. I started to have a different way of looking at the world. I started to identify myself as a victim, but also as a victim who knew that there was a way to get out of it. I didn't feel as hopeless anymore, once I started to talk to other women. I had never talked about the things that had happened to me, and incredible things had happened to me. You know, my mother had died, I had been a sexual abuse survivor and I had had a horrendous, really tragic life. Like something out of Charles Dickens. Even when I think about it now, it really blows me away. I lived in virtual isolation, I didn't talk to people, I didn't trust people, I was very sick. Very emotionally sick.

I think in general the government needs to provide a lot of services for women that they don't provide now. I think we need more women's centres. I think of all the women who've been abused as kids—if they get out of it, they're lucky. They're an anomaly, you know. It's the very tough, tenacious women who manage to evolve out of it.

Out of my $900 a month job, I pay $100 to see a feminist therapist. She has a sliding scale, and that's as low as it goes. She's the best there is. I don't begrudge her the money because I know that she needs to make a living. But this sort of therapy should be covered by medicare. It's totally unfair for poor women who are trying to better themselves and improve their self-esteem to have to pay for it. I mean, it's like the victim always pays, the victim keeps paying and paying and paying.

There is absolutely nothing in the social welfare system that gives you any motivation to get out of it. The way the system works here in this province is that it sets you up so the more fucked-up you are, the more privileges you get, so it's in your favour to act out. It was always in my favour to be an ex-psychiatric patient, drug addict, alcoholic, you know. I had access to bus passes and things that if I had been classified as a single employable person I wouldn't have had access to.

If you are a single employable person on welfare, in a province like this where there is a 10% unemployment rate, you don't have your medical paid, you don't get any help with transportation getting to and from jobs. You live on $430 a month. You don't live—you exist. You exist in some kind of subculture that forces you to stand in line-ups for food and go to food banks.

Welfare rates need to be raised, at least to the poverty level, and I don't think *that's* enough. You know, people's children are taken into care, and children in care get clothing allowances. Children in care get money to take piano lessons, all kinds of extras like that. I think moms on welfare should be provided with things, privileges for their kids. Because it is not the kids' fault that they are growing up in a poor family.

We also need job training for women. You know, my mother was forty-two when my father died. She had been a homemaker all of her life. She didn't know how to work, and she didn't have the self-esteem to work. She needed to have some kind of transition program. Money to go to school. Money to educate herself—she had never been educated. Education is part of the key, too.

There's a complete breakdown in the way that our society treats people; it's like we've lost the sense of shared responsibility for each other. When you live in a capitalist society, I don't know how you get it back. When a person's status is measured by how much they make and how well their kids are dressed and how many cars they have in the garage, that separates people so far from each other that I don't know how you ever reconcile them. People who have money and are making money feel resentful paying taxes to support people on welfare who they perceive to be lazy, good-for-nothing, useless bums who are drinking their cheques away. Money is the dividing line. I don't know how you educate people, you know, except by taking their money away and saying, "Here—experience my life for a month and see if you could live and see if you wouldn't want to kill yourself at the end of it."

I think people need to acknowledge that poverty kills. Poverty kills women, poverty kills children. Women in the community I work in die twenty-two years younger than the national average. I think what needs to be acknowledged is that poverty over a long period of time is like a slow form of death. You slowly are robbed of your self-esteem. Women are forced to steal. Women are forced to prostitution to feed their children. Their children are apprehended by the Ministry, because the women have become unfit mothers by simply trying to provide for their children in a way that they know how. Women put their lives on the line every day in the community that I work in to feed their kids and, as a result, they're raped, they're murdered...

A huge proportion of the women in jail are there for petty criminal offences—stealing, theft under $200, theft of food for their kids. The entire system is weighted against poor people.

People have to look inside themselves and survive in spite of it, and work with other people to make changes that are necessary. There's too many people who have died as a result of the kind of repression that poverty brings. For me, it's really personal. My mother committed suicide, and I really feel there was a direct correlation between the fact that she was totally impoverished and her simply giving up. In my work at the women's centre, if I can just put out a hand to somebody so she doesn't feel like she needs to give up *that* day, then we've done something.

O

222

Appendix 1

Ending Poverty: Some Ideas

Poverty is not a "fact of life." It is an outcome of specific economic and political decisions.

The Unequal Society 1985

□

A January 25, 1994, story in the *Globe & Mail* listed a number of corporations that owed $100 million or more in deferred taxes. These companies included Alcan Aluminium, Bell Canada, Canadian Pacific, Chrysler, and General Motors. End Legislated Poverty, a Vancouver anti-poverty group, said the list of corporations came to 4 pages in length, and the total in deferred taxes was over $29 billion. "Think what a difference this would make to the deficit if it were paid," wrote ELP. "Imagine how much money we could have for social programs if corporations even paid 5% interest on their deferred taxes! 5% interest on these deferred taxes would amount to about a billion and a half dollars a year."

The Long Haul
End Legislated Poverty, March 1994

□

Tax economist Neil Brooks of Osgoode Hall Law School has identified a number of tax breaks, primarily for the rich, which cost the treasury $8 billion per year. Many of these were introduced in the late 1970s. Brooks has calculated that if Canada had maintained the tax levels of the early 1970s throughout the [seventies], our national debt would have been one half of what it was by the early 1980s. A tax level similar to the European countries would create a surplus of $88 billion.

. . .

The "poverty gap," the amount of additional income that would be required to bring all Canadians above the poverty line in any given year, has become severe . . . In 1991, the poverty gap was nearly $13.4 billion . . . $13.4 billion is less than 4.7% of total government expenditure. It could easily be generated by a moderate restructuring of the taxation system. The federal government would have an additional $5.4 billion if it had held the wealthiest 10% of the population at its 1973 tax rate of 23% on all earnings and returns on investment.

**The Right to an Adequate Standard
of Living in a Land of Plenty**
Submission of NAPO and the Charter Committee
on Poverty Issues to the Committee on Economic,
Social, and Cultural Rights, May 1993.

☐

Tax reform is one economic/political decision that could be made to help end poverty in Canada. A number of organizations have developed other proposals which show that it is possible—and affordable—to put an end to poverty in Canada. Some of these proposals are described on the next pages. For information on others contact your local anti-poverty group or women's group, or write to the National Anti-Poverty Organization, 456 Rideau St., Ottawa, ON, K1N 5Z4.

☐

An Alternative Federal Budget. Published by Canadian Centre for Policy Alternatives (804 - 251 Laurier Avenue West, Ottawa, ON, K1P 5J6) and Choices (275 Broadway, 5th floor, Winnipeg, MB, R3C 4M6), 1995.

A budget based on people-oriented economic and social priorities rather than the pro-business slant of recent federal governments. (The Centre for Policy Alternatives publishes a wide range of books and pamphlets on social and economic issues.)

☐

Nancy Pollak with Kathy Sparrow, Jeff Watts, Steve Collison, and Stan de Mello. **Critical Choices, Turbulent Times: A Community Workbook on Social Programs**. Available from University of BC School of Social Work (2080 West Mall, Vancouver, BC, V6T 1Z2), 1994.

This workbook is a starting point and guide for groups that want to understand, think critically about, and act on the current debates about social policies and programs in Canada.

☐

Ecumenical Coalition for Economic Justice. **Reweaving Canada's Social Programs: From Shredded Safety Net to Social Solidarity**. Published by ECEJ (11 Madison Avenue, Toronto, ON, M5R 2S2), 1993.

This book analyzes the reasons behind the dismantling of Canada's social safety net. ECEJ, along with the five national churches that sponsor the organization, calls for an approach to social programs which gives priority to people, not profits. *Reweaving Canada's Social Programs* presents viable policy alternatives to program cuts, and outlines a new vision of social solidarity.

☐

Sherri Torjman. **The Reality Gap: Closing the Gap Between Women's Needs and Available Programs and Services**. Canadian Advisory Council on the Status of Women (Box 1541, Stn. B, Ottawa, ON, K1P 5R5), 1988.

This booklet discusses the "reality gap"—the distance between women's real-life needs and the social welfare programs and services that currently exist to meet those needs. Torjman advises women to "bridge the gap" by working to change the policies and institutions that currently fail to serve women. *The Reality Gap* does not deal directly with the question "where will the money come from," but suggests that shifting priorities would reallocate money for women's needs and programs.

☐

Lucy Alderson, Melanie Conn, Janet Donald, Molly Harrington, and Leslie Kemp. **Counting Ourselves In: A Women's Community Economic Development Handbook**. Published by WomenFutures (217 - 1956 West Broadway, Vancouver, BC, V6J 1Z2) and SPARC (106 - 2182 West 12 Ave., Vancouver, BC, V6K 2N4), 1993.

This handbook outlines a step-by-step process for women to meet and discuss ways to improve the quality of their communities and their lives. Many examples of women's community economic development projects are described (creating affordable housing, starting community businesses, setting up barter networks, doing research and education), and there are suggestions for other projects.

☐

As I updated this book, the federal Liberal government began a review of Canada's social programs with an eye to revamping the system. Groups like the National Anti-Poverty Organization, National Action Committee on the Status of Women, Canadian Advisory Council on the Status of Women and others made presentations to the committee, arguing for the maintenance of social programs and outlining how they can be funded. These presentations are available on request from the organizations (their addresses are in the following section).

In the spring of 1995 the review was put on the back burner, and on February 27 the government released a budget that continued the slashing of support programs for women, the poor, children and others. It is going to be even harder to qualify for UI, there will be new restrictions on welfare that could turn it into workfare or a low-wage subsidy for employers, and transfer payments that help the provinces pay for health, education and welfare programs were reduced by $7 billion.

Then on March 17, funding for the Canadian Advisory Council on the Status of Women was cut completely. CACSW was a government-appointed but independent research body that studied women's issues and advised the government and the public on topics like child care, reproductive health, paid and unpaid work, violence against women and women's educational needs. I've used CACSW materials in my research for this book.

When the Liberals were elected in 1993 they said their priority was to create jobs for all Canadians; now their priority seems to be to continue the Conservatives' cutting of social programs. Women must make their voices heard in this debate.

□

According to Statistics Canada . . .
50% of the debt is due to tax breaks for upper income earners and corporations;
44% of the debt is due to high interest rates;
4% of the debt is due to general program spending;
2% of the debt can be attributed to social programs.

Statistics Canada 1991
(quoted in the Action Canada Network's
Action Dossier, Fall 1994)

Appendix 2
Anti-Poverty and Women's Groups

There are many more anti-poverty, welfare rights and women's groups in Canada than are listed here. To find a group in your area, contact the National Anti-Poverty Organization at 316 - 256 King Edward Ave., Ottawa, ON, K1N 7M1, or the National Action Committee on the Status of Women, 234 Edmonton Ave. East, Toronto, ON, M4P 1K5. The backbone of this list came from *Counting Ourselves In: A Women's Community Economic Development Handbook* produced by WomenFutures and SPARC. I also had help compiling the list from NAPO, ELP, and Vancouver Status of Women. Thanks to you all!

British Columbia

**Bread & Roses
Women's Centre**
Box 453
Kitimat, BC, V8C 2R9

**Campbell River Women's
Resource Society**
457 10 Ave.
Campbell River, BC, V9W 4E4

Chetwynd Women's Centre
Box 626
Chetwynd, BC, V0C 1J0

**Comox Valley
Women's Centre**
Box 3292
Courtenay, BC, V9N 5N4

**Downtown Eastside
Women's Centre**
44 East Cordova St.
Vancouver, BC, V6A 1K2

End Legislated Poverty
211 - 456 West Broadway
Vancouver, BC, V5Y 1R3

**Fort St. John Women's
Resource Society**
102 - 10343 - 100 Ave.
Fort St. John, BC, V1J 1Y8

**Howe Sound
Women's Centre**
Box 2052
Squamish, BC, V0N 3G0

**Kamloops Women's
Resource Centre**
7E - 750 Cottonwood Ave.
Kamloops, BC, V2B 3X2

**Kelowna Women's
Resource Centre**
107 - 347 Leon Ave.
Kelowna, BC, V1Y 8C7

**Nanaimo Women's
Resources Society**
219 - 285 Prideaux
Nanaimo, BC, V9R 2N2

Quesnel Women's Centre
690 McLean St.
Quesnel, BC, V2J 2P6

**Social Planning and
Research Council**
108 - 2182 West 12 Ave.
Vancouver, BC, V6K 2N4

Vancouver Lesbian Centre
876 Commercial Dr.
Vancouver, BC, V5L 3W5

**Vancouver Society for
Immigrant and Visible
Minority Women**
204 - 2524 Cypress St.
Vancouver, BC, V6J 4W2

Vancouver Status of Women
301 - 1720 Grant St.
Vancouver, BC, V5L 2X7

**Woman to Woman
Global Strategies**
2524 Cypress St.
Vancouver, BC, V6J 4W2

WomenFutures CED Society
217 - 1956 West Broadway
Vancouver, BC, V6J 1Z2

Rest of Canada

**Alberta Status of Women
Action Committee**
10 - 9930 - 106 St.
Edmonton, AB, T5K 1E2

**Boyle Street Community
Services Co-op**
9420 - 102 Ave.
Edmonton, AB, T5J 4B2

**Calgary Immigrant
Women's Centre**
230 - 1035 - 7 Ave. SW
Calgary, AB, T2P 3E9

**Calgary Status of Women
Action Committee**
319 - 223 - 12 Ave. SW
Calgary, AB, T2R 0G9

Poverty Focus Group
c/o John Howard Society
200 - 1010 - 1 St. SW
Calgary, AB, T2R 1K4

**Aboriginal Women's
Council of Saskatchewan**
206 - 1311 Central Ave.
Prince Albert, SK, S6V 4W2

Equal Justice for All
325 Avenue E South
Saskatoon, SK, S7M 1S2

**Métis Women of
Saskatchewan Inc.**
219 Robin Cres.
Saskatoon, SK, S7L 6M8

**National Organization of
Immigrant and Visible
Minority Women of
Canada/Canadian Congress
of Black Women**
79 Murphy Cres.
Regina, SK, S4X 1S6

Rural Women Resource
Box 127
Oxbow, SK, S0C 2B0

**Saskatchewan Action
Committee, Status of
Women**
2343 Cornwall St.
Regina, SK, S4P 2L4

**Saskatchewan Anti-Poverty
Legal Rights Committee**
c/o 1820 Quebec St.
Regina, SK, S4P 1J5

**Manitoba Action for the
Status of Women**
16 - 222 Osborne St. S
Winnipeg, MB, R3L 1Z3

**Manitoba Anti-Poverty
Organization**
365 McGee St.
Winnipeg, MB, R3G 3M5

Métis Women of Manitoba
Wanless, MB, R0B 1T0

Parkdale Status of Women
Box 23
Dauphin, MB, R7N 2T9

**Thompson Action
Committee on the
Status of Women**
Box 722
Thompson, MB, R8N 1N5

**Canadian Centre for Policy
Alternatives**
804 - 251 Laurier Ave. West
Ottawa, ON, K1P 5J6

**Canadian Council on
Social Development**
55 Parkdale Ave.
Ottawa, ON, K1Y 4G1

Citizens for Public Justice
229 College St.
Toronto, ON, M5T 1R4

Count Us in Project M.A.W.
(Campaign to recognize
women's unpaid work in the
home and as volunteers)
Box 4104, Stn. E
Ottawa, ON, K1S 5B1

**Ecumenical Coalition for
Economic Justice**
11 Madison Ave.
Toronto ON, M5R 2S2

**Low Income
Families Together**
301 - 183 Bathurst St.
Toronto, ON, M5T 2R7

**National Action Committee
on the Status of Women**
234 Edmonton Ave. E.
Toronto, ON, M4P 1K5

**National Anti-Poverty
Organization**
316 - 256 King Edward Ave.
Ottawa, ON, K1N 7M1

National Council of Welfare
Jeanne Mance Building
Ottawa, ON, K1A 0K9

**Native Women's
Resource Centre**
245 Gerrard St. E.
Toronto, ON, M5A 2G1

**Ontario Coalition
Against Poverty**
249 Sherbourne St.
Toronto, ON, M5A 2R9

**Ontario Immigrant and
Visible Minority Women's
Organizations**
394 Euclid Ave.
Toronto, ON, M6G 2S9

**Front commun des
personnes assistées sociales**
1222 rue St. Hubert
Montréal, PQ, H2L 3Y7

**Québec Native
Women's Association**
1450 City Councillors St.
Montreal, PQ, H3A 2E5

**l'R des centres de
femmes du Québec**
4206 St. Denis
Montreal, PQ, H2J 2K8

**Fredericton Anti-Poverty
Organization**
242 Gibson St.
Fredericton, NB, E3A 4E3

**New Brunswick
Anti-Poverty Association**
Box 6446, Stn. A
Saint John, NB, E2L 4R8

**New Brunswick Native
Women's Council**
65 Brunswick St.
Fredericton, NB

**Advisory Council on the
Status of Women**
Box 859
Amherst, NS, B4H 4B9

**Caring About People
in Poverty**
60 Ellenvale Ave.
Dartmouth, NS, B2W 2W5

Congress of Black Women
1935 Highway 7, SS 2
Suite 10, Comp 10
East Preston, NS, B2H 3Y2

Nova Scotia Action Committee on the Status of Women
Box 745
Halifax, NS, B3J 2T3

Aboriginal Women's Association of PEI
Box 145
Lennox Island, PEI, C0B 1P0

ALERT
Box 2322
Charlottetown, PEI, C1A 8C1

L'Association des femmes Acadiennes et Franco-phones de la region Evangeline
Wellington, PEI, C0B 2E0

PEI Advisory Council on the Status of Women
Box 2000
Charlottetown, PEI, C1A 7N8

Women's Network
3 Queen St.
Charlottetown, PEI, C1A 7K4

Group Against Poverty
Box 1574, Stn. C
St. John's, NF, A1C 5P3

Newfoundland Advisory Council on the Status of Women
136 Lemarchant Rd.
St. John's, NF, A1C 2H3

Newfoundland & Labrador Federation of Co-operatives
Box 13369, Stn. A
St. John's, NF, A1B 4B7

Women's Enterprise Bureau
85 Water St.
St. John's, NF, A1C 1A5

Native Women's Association of the NWT
Box 2321
Yellowknife, NWT, X1A 2P7

Pauktuutit Inuit Women's Association
804 - 200 Elgin St.
Ottawa, ON, K2P 1L5

Status of Women Council of the NWT
Box 1320
Yellowknife, NWT, X1A 2L9

Yellowknife Women's Centre
Box 2645
Yellowknife, NWT, X1A 2P9

Victoria Faulkner Women's Centre
8 - 106 Main St.
Whitehorse, YT, Y1A 2A8

Russell Kelly

Sheila Baxter has been active in the anti-poverty movement since 1970. She was a founder of Chez Doris, a drop-
in centre for street women in Montreal. Since moving to
Vancouver she has been active in the downtown eastside
and west end on poverty issues. Sheila has had three books
published — *No Way to Live* (1988), *Under the Viaduct:
Homeless in Beautiful B.C.* (1991), and *A Child is Not a Toy:
Voices of Children in Poverty* (1993) — and she is currently at
work on her next book. She is in demand as a speaker on
poverty issues and writing, and has given workshops using
drama to educate students about poverty. Sheila is a single
mother of four adult children and eight grandchildren.